PSYCHOBIOGRAPHIC APPROACH TO PSYCHOTHERAPY:

A Study of the Power Structure of Psychotherapy

PSYCHOBIOGRAPHIC APPROACH TO PSYCHOTHERAPY: A STUDY OF THE POWER STRUCTURE OF PSYCHOTHERAPY

Herzel Yerushalmi, Ph.D.

PSYCHOSOCIAL PRESS
MADISON, CONNECTICUT

Library of Congress Cataloging-in-Publication Data

Yerushalmi, Herzel.
 Psychobiographic approach to psychotherapy : a study of the power structure of psychotherapy / Herzel Yerushalmi.
     p.   cm.
 Includes bibliographical references and index.
 ISBN 1-887841-12-1
  1. Psychotherapist and patient.   2. Psychotherapy—Philosophy.
 3. Client-centered psychotherapy.   4. Oppression (Psychology)
 5. Control (Psychology) 6. Power (Social sciences)   I. Title.
 RC480.8.Y47   1997
 616.89'14—dc21   97-21398
                                                        CIP

Manufactured in the United States of America

For
my wife and companion, Shlomit, and my children
Gilat, Eyal, and Revital.
To
my father, Yossof Ourshalimian, and my mother, Janet,
and to
all who helped me to understand life.

Contents

PART III
Psychobiographic Psychotherapy

Acknowledgments

I owe a deep debt of gratitude to Mary Willson Williams, Ph.D., for her firm belief in the value of my writing, for her personal support and encouragement, and for her invaluable suggestions and editorial commentary. This work would have been still in its infancy without her selfless help as a mentor and teacher.

Over the years I have been very fortunate to meet teachers whose guidance, thinking, and personality indirectly have shaped this book. Gedon Medini, Ph.D.: for showing me, among other things, the psychotherapeutic virtues of a cup of hot soup; Masha Mishkinski, M.A.: for reminding me not to forget the "heart and soul"; the late Yehuda Fried, M.D.: for encouraging me not to give up on anyone; Zvi Giora, Ph.D.: for an unforgettable intellectual experience in a year-long course at Tel-Aviv University; Gila Ofer, M.A., my first individual supervisor: for personally demonstrating to a struggling novice what empathy is; Rosemarie Kopka, M.A.: for the great privilege of meeting a true humanist.

Other teachers and colleagues have directly helped shape this book. Among the most important are Noel Markwell, Ph.D. and Lawrence J. Ryan, Ph.D. of The Union Institute, Gay Hartell-Lloyd, Ph.D., Victor Solomon, Ph.D., Michael Trumbull, Ph.D., and Thomas Edward Rugh, Ph.D. They provided personal warmth, support, intellectual critique, and thoughtful remarks. Shirley Frank, Ph.D., has done intensive editorial work.

Many individuals helped me to write this book in other ways. Some as friends: Yussef Sakhai, M.D., and Samuel Bar-or who resisted my temptations to change my natural course of study at a time of personal crisis. I wish to extend my heartfelt appreciation to Nina A. Weiner for her warm support of my struggle in the world of ideas. Nehemia Friedlander, Ph.D. and Arie Nadler, Ph.D. made possible my professional life and to whom I owe special gratitude for accepting me for study to the department of psychology at Tel-Aviv University.

Two other people deserve special gratitude. The first, Margaret Emery, Ph.D., of Psychosocial Press for her careful attention to the meaning of my book, for her final editing, and for seeing this book into production and publication.

The second is my wife, Shlomit Mona Yerushalmi. She mothered my ideas from their irresolute inception until their much more than nine months of painstaking delivery. She has made precious contribution to this book as research associate and as an empathic intellectual critic. To her I owe the rather creative part of my life cycle.

Last but certainly not least, I wish to thank those individuals with whom I have been privileged to work in the therapeutic conversations, and whose partnership made my learning possible.

PART I

INTRODUCTION

Introduction

My writing is about life. It is a study of psychological life. Naturally I begin this introductory chapter with a life: mine. There are moments of choice which, even if they pass by unnoticed, dramatically symbolize the amalgamation and culmination of numerous and manifold personal dynamic forces and motives. The moment I chose to become a psychology major, I decided in favor of (1) loyal, continual dedication to internal self-search of my total experience in my efforts to weave meanings in and out of issues concerning human life, and (2) grounding those issues, pertaining to human life, in life itself.

Out of what ground of concerns, earned knowledge, and personal and professional experience did the present topic evolve? What stand out as critical incidents in my life which created at first puzzlement, then discontent, and at last intense curiosity and passion to inquire about and study them? In rewriting this piece of personal history I aspire to state and elucidate the key questions that have profoundly affected my investigations, and which I believe hold possibilities for scientific knowledge and social meaning.

In retrospect, it seems to me that my whole academic endeavor was characterized by ingenuous assumptions. I was naive. In fact, for reasons to be touched upon later, inwardly I fought against letting go of my naiveté. I thought that by entering college I would be furnished with possibilities for a trenchant search for deep truths about human conditions. I was sure university would help me to complete the task of building up my soul.

After all, this is what education is about, isn't it? Aren't we, the students of life, interested in questions concerning three basic matters: God, love, and death? (I might also add to the equation the element of money, but we will leave that aside for the time being.)

I was lucky. My grade point average was not high enough for me to apply to the school of psychology. In a hectic search to make some sense of the world and my place in it, I thought that it would be just naturally logical that I should want to inquire into how the social systems we are living in came into existence. I found myself reading feverishly through hundreds of years of historical development. I discovered time and again that thousands of people early in the dawn of history and for many ages afterwards subdued their freedom of thought, their independence of thought and feelings, to some figure, dominant and powerful, out of some sort of misery and in favor of an idea, a very material idea indeed, that of *hope*—the German Nazi movement being the embodiment of this recurring symptom at its extremity.

It was, and still is, fascinating and overwhelming, to see how so many people so many times are voluntarily brainwashed into believing in an illusion. After all, we should admit that these are the most massive change processes known to humans. Let me explain. There exists some sort of misery or distress which elicits some sort of hope, which can at times be a very dangerous emotion, and which in turn causes a shift in the belief system, that is, adoption of some sort of illusion(s) as a remedy to that distress. Later, in another discipline, I came to understand that there was another word for this phenomenon: placebo, and the suggestion that leads the person to believe in the illusion that a particular effect will occur. But let us delay this discussion for the moment.

So, I found myself in history. The subject matter of my hungry spirit eventually and inevitably was the masses. History is not interested in the individual unless he or she is "somebody," a persona. Elsewhere I have elaborated on other reasons for my disappointment with the study of history. Here I want to be more specific, more personal, and less intellectual. For a while I was numbed, while strolling leisurely through the pages of the glamorous lives and spectacular castles of the political celebrities of the ruling elites. Gradually I came to realize that two deadly plagues, War and Class, have been with us ever since the first civilization, and confront our civilization with a challenge today. The eminent historian Arnold J. Toynbee (1948) observed that of 20 or so civilizations known to modern Western historians, all except our own appear to be dead or moribund, and when we diagnose each case, we invariably find that the cause of death has been either war or class or some combination of the two.

But under whose pain does this tragic, never-ending display of power exert itself? How is it that those who choreographed and waged wars have been given titles like "The Great," and similar other superlatives, while those common people who by common sense have opposed wars have been ostracized and outlawed? Concomitantly I came to realize that war is inflicted on many, regardless of whether they are in favor or in opposition, engaged in or disengaged in class wars. There is war everywhere, between countries, within countries, on the streets, in neighborhoods, and within homes. It seemed to me that first and foremost it is the reality which is abusive—to the anonymous individual. As time passed, in efforts to make history not only one of a series of discourses about the world but also and primarily one about the material world, the human condition, I started to plunge more deeply into the life of the Greco-Roman plebe, the medieval peasant, the modern proletarian, and those in the postmodern privatized middle-class, dragging behind them vast layers of disenfranchised homeless–worldless individuals.

Does history have any use? During the middle and late 1970s, many empiricist historians still believed their discipline could be a science aiming at objectivity and facts. They were committed to the idea that somehow the past can be recreated objectively. Others believed that historical truth is relative, always varying with the time and place of the observer. The empiricists believe that one can and should detect biases and expunge them by scrupulous inquiry into "what the sources say." The relativists claim that the sources are mute, that we can attend to the same source and still come out with different accounts, that there are as many histories as historians, history being narration and interpretation. History, the latter argue, is never value-free and always takes a position. We can summarize the essence of these controversies in one question: Is a scientific history possible or is history essentially an art?

There was no denial of the above duality. Fierce and flaming discussions, characterized by intellectual honesty, echoed in the lengthy corridors of humanities departments and in the classrooms.

With these debates anchored firmly in my personality makeup, I stepped hopefully into psychology. What motivated the change? I needed "sources" that were not mute. I was no longer interested in the masses, but in the single person. Though history in those days was introducing the notion of empathy, roughly meaning to see the past from its own point of view, I was craving for empathy in understanding the present from its own perspective. History is essentially an intellectual and at times also a spiritual endeavor, and in those days I thought that psychology might strike a better balance among intellect-emotion-spirit. So there I was, in psychology, anticipating a different and more comprehensive response in my pursuit of making sense of the world, of my place in it, and of understanding the human predicament.

But by how much and in what ways I was wrong is the subject of my discussion. The standard menu awaiting the student of psychology did not spare me. Psychology is a very difficult subject to teach, particularly if one has no teaching education because there is no awareness that teaching by itself serves "the human body of knowledge." Aren't we—the walking bodies on earth, and not solely our brains or the number of our published pages—the subjects and carriers of this mythicized knowledge? Then, how many passionate, resourceful, and soulful teaching professors were there who as a matter of intellectual honesty debated with us, the mindful, curious learners and students of life, the basic essential questions and controversies in our fresh and blooming discipline? You could count them all on one hand.

So we were taught to believe we were in the realm of science. That meant statistics, and more statistics, and more on methodology, and, in order not to leave room for mistakes, a very specific kind of methodology; and rats demonstrating learning capabilities in UPS-type

boxes; perception becoming a matter of location–dislo-
cation of prisms, and so on. Where have God, love, and
death vanished to, I was painfully crying. The response
was harsh and definitive: psychology is experimental, a
hypotheticodeductive method.

What did I know about psychology prior to majoring
in psychology? My first acquaintance with psychology
was during my adolescent years. Those are turbulent
years when most of us ask the right questions, and then
are sometimes tamed and trained to go for the wrong
answers, or simply forget the questions as if they were
relevant only then, at that particular developmental
stage. Well, now I am middle aged, married to a woman
I love, raising three adolescents I love, and still thinking
and feeling about love and sex and their vicissitudes.

I read Erich Fromm's *The Art of Loving* (1956), and
then *Escape from Freedom* (1941), and *Socialist Humanism—An International Symposium* (1967), and later
Manes Sperber's *Alfred Adler oder Das Elend der Psychologie* (1933/1972).

I want to quote something I underlined from the last
book: "We should view psychology as a disassembling
discipline, which is partly a science, partly philosophy,
and above all, and maybe primarily, an art, which is hard
to define." I was thinking of psychology as the utmost
illumination of human efforts in pursuit of integration.
Was I naive? Of course I was. Was I wrong? Yes and no.
I was wrong because *academic* psychology was not what
I thought it was. I was not wrong because that is what I
believe *psychology* is, an integration. Am I a scientist? Yes
and no. I appreciate the pursuit of objectivity and its
quantitative methodologies in our efforts to make reli-
able sense of the universe, but as a clinical psychologist
who is interested in the microuniverse, I am above all

and primarily, interested in the single person and the unique qualities each possesses. I am a scientist–artist psychologist.

Now you are certainly asking yourself: Okay, but how does all this relate to your scientific–artistic research? I would like to ask for your patience, because my point is building up gradually, step by step, as with the person who turns to psychotherapy after a long, gradual process of building up distress.

And, in general, distress is our subject. It is obvious that I was distressed with disappointment. There were gaps and disparities. My informal knowledge of psychology did not quite match the "reality" of the study of psychology. What I propose here as a general outline is that the *other* person (referred to in this book as the Other)—for reasons to be discussed later, I refrain from and disapprove of such terms as *patient* or *client*—who seeks help via psychotherapy might go through a similar process of disappointment characterized by disparity of expectations. Further, I never lost faith in psychology, not personally, nor as a vital human science for human beings. I kept on crying—in two senses of the word—for double meaning, and fighting for my views. I am afraid that this is not what happens with the other person confronting the same predicament. The individual who seeks psychotherapy is often going to be, and actually is, giving up. In this respect psychology is perpetuating a human predicament. Now let us turn to an explication of what the specific nature of this predicament, or disparity of expectations is, and what, I might say tragically, is being perpetuated.

Gradually I came to feel there was something missing, and something else that was overpresent. I was

never mad, clinically speaking, and the DSM-IV reaf-
firms this impression. For me, madness, like any other
form of mental suffering, was simply about suffering. I
moved on to clinical psychology because I was trying to
understand the possible meanings of these and other
sufferings. In this respect I conceived the meaning of
interpretation. I was convinced, naively in retrospect,
that psychology, the profession of psychology—definitely clinical psychology—was about the humanization
of human suffering, whether one has gone mad or not.
No entity holds a patent on suffering. Here I was, in
the temperate rooms of the ivory tower, discussing psychopathology, and more psychopathology, in an abstract, lifeless manner.

I should remind you that we were supposedly the
intellectual elite of the human race. Everything is built
around status symbols—on which I will expand much
more later—that are intended to enhance our image in
our own and the public's eye. There is no need to specify in detail the prerequisites for acceptance to graduate
studies in clinical psychology. It is so flattering to our
image—those of us who have been admitted to the
ranks of the privileged minority—that it has become
introjected deep inside us, away from any access by our
scrutinizing awareness. I remember myself sitting non-
temperately there and imagining about schizophrenia,
psychopathy, and the host of categories in the textbooks. I passed all the exams with very good grades. I
could lecture on schizophrenia without knowing anything about a schizophrenic. Who is this person who
hallucinates being a prophet? I knew nothing about the
individual, but a lot about his or her disease. As a not-
so-young, but still young, member of the profession, and
definitely fresh, I believed that all these categorizations

were a prologue which eventually would lead to the main course of furnishing an appropriate, scientifically measured procedure for alleviating human sufferings. And science, I was to believe, could never be cruel; that is, it could never use power inappropriately.

I enrolled in an advanced course in psychopathology which was being held in a prestigious mental health hospital. Here I encountered one of the most astonishing insights of my professional life, which has continued to impose on my tranquillity ever since. I noticed that many of the "patients" had come to the hospital either reluctantly or by force. Many of those, I discovered later in my clinical work there and at other mental hospitals, who had come with some sense of free will, regretted it later. Lora, an attractive 23-year-old woman who was diagnosed as paranoid schizophrenic, and who had spent 4 years in a closed ward when I met her for therapy, described this disturbing fact vividly and, believe me, very painfully: "I was so lonely. I thought that they were coming to kill me. I was frightened to death. Then they [her parents and the nurse] told me that if I came here [psychiatric hospital] I would be safe; that they would treat me well, you know, as a human being. [*Me: Do you mean they would understand you?*] Yes, believe in me. [*Me: That you are so scared?*] Yes, but they did not, they tied me up. [*Me: What did you understand?*] I understood that they were also my *enemy*."

Psychology and the related professions are obliged to confront this question of ally versus foe; otherwise we will always be on the defensive, even if we do our best—and we actually do it very successfully—to disguise it. We can ennoble ourselves, and bestow upon ourselves the most adored emblems and honorary titles; neverthe-less, this profession will not truly get legitimized in the eyes of the public and those who need its services unless it becomes a benefactor, and not an enemy.

The reader might dispute the novelty of this idea. Thomas Szasz and R. D. Laing long ago criticized the repressive use of psychiatry. Szasz distinguishes between what he calls *institutional psychiatry,* practiced by state physicians, and *contractual psychiatry,* practiced with vol-untary patients who actively seek a therapist's help. He believed that institutional psychiatry is a formidable po-litical weapon and that contractual psychiatry is not; that humanization of the profession will be achieved when we get rid of institutional psychiatry and adhere to a nonmedical role for psychiatrists who deal only with voluntary patients.

Seymour Halleck (1971) demonstrates how psychia-try might be, and in fact is, politically oppressive. He is convinced that Szasz's distinction is a false one: that any kind of psychiatric intervention might have repressive, or liberating, consequences for individual patients.

On the face of it, Halleck is at variance with Szasz, but not so. Halleck agrees that in fact there exists such an entity as nonconstitutional psychiatry/psychology. This distinction, together with the one mentioned above, is in my view a false one. Any kind of psychiatric/ psychological intervention is constitutional, ingrained deeply in the prevailing political–economical system. Furthermore, the notion that there is such a phenome-non as the *voluntary patient* is still another false one. The very concept of *patient* implies a person who is at physical or mental dis-ease, who resorts to therapy, med-ical or psychological, in order to relieve the source of that dis-ease. People do not seek a doctor to help better their health, physical or mental, without having an apparent symptom. For one to knock on the door and plead that, "I want to understand myself and the world around me," is a rarity. People are forced to therapy by symptoms which inflict suffering on themselves or on others or both. In other words, people resort to therapy when they are at an impasse, physically or psychologically.

For the time being I would like to pose these questions: Why are there not people who claim therapy at will? Why are there only "patients"? Are these "patients" the only people in need of therapy?

Roughly classified, there seem to exist three large groups of people who seek some kind of therapeutic intervention. The first group is comprised of those who are designated mentally ill and suffer from some kind of psychosis. They usually do not seek therapy and are forced into it either by a relative or by circumstances. The second group consists of the classic "neurotics." They usually wait until their troubles have reached a climax, their situation is bearable no longer, and they can take no more. For them, "The waters are come in even unto the soul." A small portion of these "neurotics" possibly will find their way to some sort of psychological therapy. Many others—and the magnitude of this phenomenon will be my concern later—will resort to everything imaginable except psychotherapy. The third large group, which will be at the center of my scrutiny, consists of what might be termed the *scientific* group. In this group we find all the prospective practitioners of psychotherapy: psychiatrists, psychologists from various schools, counselors, social workers, etc. Do they volunteer and apply for psychotherapy at will? In

fact, this group resembles the neurotic one in every aspect, but its members prefer to be perceived as different. An example might illustrate my point: I was once
an intern in an outpatient institution affiliated with a
prestigious university, where we were assigned to group
supervision. The supervisor introduced herself briefly
and then turned to us. After a short round, she asked
if any of us had gone through "counseling or psychotherapy," and the interns answered, each in turn, making complimentary remarks on the virtues of counseling
in regard to their professional growth. She phrased the
question in a manner that could be interpreted in either
of two ways. The interns preceding me chose to relate
to the learning aspect of their counseling experience,
circumventing indications of any kind of serious distress. In other words, they were implicitly saying: As a
result of my counseling experience I have become a
better therapist, and I am on my way to becoming a
professional therapist; I have gone to counseling not
because I was wrecked with any kind of *psychopathology*
but because I wanted to learn how to deal with my own
issues. Later, when out of reach of the supervisor's supervisory grid, we joked about our "personal growth
group," as I used to refer to it humorously. But at the
time I did not feel humorous. It was my turn and I was
in distress. I decided to head the other way by telling
the group that I went through therapy because of being
in emotional distress, hoping to gain some understanding about my doings, and thus alleviating my suffering,
or at least some of it. Then, believing in the principle
of mutuality, I turned to the supervisor, to her surprise
of course, and asked if she had been in therapy—with
an emphasis on *therapy* and not on counseling. "Yes,"
she replied, with an air of academic significance in her

tone, "I have been through *analysis*," and then she made that important move, surely in her opinion, that set her apart forever from the rest of the apprentices: "There I learned how to do *therapy*." Therapy, this time, and not analysis—liberating us from any shred of doubt about her diverse dexterity.

Donald P. Spence (1982), in writing about the problem of language in examining the dialectic between facts and constructions of the past, notes:

> "[T]he names for things are not exactly lying around, waiting to be picked up and placed into sentences; every word marks a specific decision by the author and every sentence represents a particular overall combination of these words. The author is faced with the problem of how to express his view of the world in a string of words that will convey the same representation to someone who may have shared none of the experience. (p. 40)

He quotes Benjamin Lee Whorf, who found that words influence how we see the world; and our choice of categories to write about will determine which words are relevant.

I claim that the view of the world expressed by the "supervisor" in the example above is representative of many others in the realm of psychotherapy; that mental health practitioners are using a mutual, class-oriented, private language for people who do not share the same language, which is strange to them, and yet who do share the same *experience*; that some very specific decisions and choices of categories are being made that are in fact detrimental to the very nature of our profession and indeed facilitate the perpetuation of a human predicament.

Let us examine in detail this worldview and its grave implications. A distinction is being made between worldviews of human beings characterizing different *systems* of psychotherapy, and worldviews characterizing human beings comprising our profession, no matter which system they adhere to. In other words, *all* the current systems of psychotherapy share the same underlying worldview. Later we will address the question of how and where—in theory, in practice, or both—this worldview is manifested.

Turning to the examples above we can delineate several premises or categories comprising this worldview. These will be the subject of the following chapters, and they will be noted together with their opposites, which comprise the frame of the psychobiographic approach to psychotherapy.

CHAPTER ONE

Separatism vs. Egalitarianism

In the therapeutic setting, the language we use serves to set us apart from the other party, the so-called "patient" or *Other* as I prefer to call him or her. This same maneuver is used also to separate us within our own profession. As a segment, we try to convey the impression that we were born normal, brought up and developed within a normal range; or, if there were some unfortunate lags, we had "worked" on them through "therapy" or, preferably, "analysis," which connotes a higher location on the status ladder. But why have we chosen in the first place, this time absolutely at will, to pursue a career in psychology, clinical social work, or psychiatry? We will recruit all the possible arguments only to throw a haze over the real, the very personal, and very intimate. Examination of some autobiographies and application of text analysis might elucidate this issue.

Spurgeon English's "How I Found My Way to Psychiatry" (1972) confronts the readers with this puzzling ambiguity. After finishing his internship, English was wondering what course his career in medicine would take. He had thought of going into general practice in his home territory and also of a career in surgery. "However, with my illness [pulmonary tuberculosis] I felt I should enter some specialty in which I could control my working hours." Out of the possibilities of dermatology, radiology, and psychiatry, he chose psychiatry. One might wonder how English, who is very familiar with the psychoanalytic literature and furthermore had gone through psychoanalytic "training" and/or "analysis," ignores a matter of such common knowledge both in psychoanalysis and in history as manifest content versus latent content. Should the scrutinizing mind believe in the priority of the vague motive cited by him? Why, especially, psychiatry out of the three options? English does not furnish us with any explicit answer to these disturbing questions. The curious and obstinate reader might find the reason by going a few lines back from the one quoted above. Here you discover that just before wondering about his career course, English was the victim of a third attack of pulmonary tuberculosis, resulting in his being shipped off to a sanitarium where he remained for 15 months, and that: "During this time I encountered my first depression and my first over-preoccupation with my self, my health, and my future" (p. 82). Further back still, you learn that he was raised by a "neurotic mother" who was humorless, overserious, overreligious, and pessimistic; tended to fear the outside world; never enjoyed being the wife of a farmer, his father; was distrustful of the morality and good intentions of everyone in the surrounding town and country; and that only by avoiding involvement with her was he able "to possess a few emotionally healthy attributes" by the time he reached the age of 21. However, English was told that at around the age of 2 or 3 he was prone to severe nightmares during which he seemed to be falling off the world into outer space—a sensation that was accompanied by terrifying emotions.

One might wonder about the reason for this displacement of the manifest with the latent, this ambiguity. Again, the text furnishes us with an answer which, I contend, is a general rule prevalent in today's scientific wisdom and practice: In the preface, English declares that he begins this assignment "with feelings of both trepidation and pleasure" (p. 78). The former is due to the well-known fact that excessive self-revelation in print exposes one to the varied ambivalent feelings of the world at large. Differently worded, English's "trepidation" stems from a fear of being pathographized, stigmatized.

Stolorow and Atwood (1979) argue that the theories of Sigmund Freud, Carl Jung, Otto Rank, and Wilhelm Reich were based in important ways on interpretations of themselves which were then formulated as more general theories of human personality and psychotherapy. Ebbinghaus' studies of himself were crucial in developing his theories of memory (Dukes, 1965). The question I raise concerns the motifs underneath the need for such self-interpretations. And I argue that the same personal motifs are shared by all parties involved in the practice of psychotherapy, but that only a few maintain enough courage to admit to it and to make efforts to transform this acknowledgment into a humanistic and egalitarian interpersonal interaction. Carl Rogers exemplified one of these very few. He said:

> As I look back, I realize that my interest in interviewing and in therapy certainly grew in part out of my early loneliness. Here was a socially approved way of getting really close to individuals and thus filling some of the hungers I had undoubtedly felt. The therapeutic interview also offered a chance of becoming close without having to go through what was to me a long and painful

process of gradual and deepening acquaintance. (Rogers, 1980, p. 34)

Jung, on the other hand, is precursor to Spurgeon English. Jung's life history is replete with the nonordinary (Hall & Nordby, 1973; Jung, 1961). His mother suffered from emotional disorders and depressions; his parents had marital problems ever since the child could remember, and they slept in separate bedrooms. Jung shared a bedroom with his father who was an irritable person, and difficult to get along with. When conditions became unbearable, Jung sought refuge in the attic, where he had a companion to console him for hours—a manikin he had carved from a piece of wood. During childhood he developed fainting spells of psychological etiology, and once he missed more than 6 months of school. He was an introvert throughout his life, and did not show much interest in people. While Rogers utilized his loneliness as a vehicle for relatedness, Jung, who also as a child and youth suffered from almost unendurable loneliness, was paralyzed by it: "Thus the pattern of my relationship to the world was already prefigured: today as then I am a solitary" (Jung, 1961, p. 58).

Jung's father died a year after Jung had entered the university, and during his third year, Jung was trying to decide whether to specialize in surgery or internal medicine. The following summer he experienced some occult phenomena, and he even began attending seances and table turnings. He was on the verge of devoting himself to internal medicine when something happened "which removed all my doubts concerning my future career" (Jung, 1961, p. 129). And what is that "something," you may wonder?: a textbook on psychiatry. Was it his first encounter with this subject? Of course not. He had attended psychiatric lectures and clinics, and he was currently attending one which he found not very stimulating; he also had firsthand "experience of asylums" to which his father was confined, but "this was not calculated to prepossess me in favor of psychiatry" (p. 129).

What, then, in that textbook of Krafft-Ebing, he was reading, prepossessed him, "in violent reaction," in favor of psychiatry? Since Jung himself admits that Krafft-Ebing's textbook did not differ essentially from other books of the time, there should have been something personally and subjectively meaningful: "Beginning with the preface, I read: 'It is probably due to the peculiarity of the subject and its incomplete state of development that psychiatric textbooks are stamped with a more or less subjective character.' " This "subjective character" and naming psychoses as "diseases of the personality" a few lines later struck Jung "like a bolt of lightening" (Hall & Nordby, 1973): "Here alone the two currents of my interest could flow together and in a united stream dig their own bed. Here was the empirical field common to biological and spiritual facts, which I had everywhere sought and nowhere found. Here at last was the place where the collision of nature and spirit became a reality" (p. 130). Jung transforms the subjective and personal into the objective and general, contrary to his own teaching, when it comes to subjects that concern him and his own personality. Jung's life history is the epitome of a psychiatric textbook. In psychiatry he found, at last, a place where his own nature and his own spirit could potentially coalesce and become a comprehensible reality. So it was with Jung, and so it is with the other person who resorts to therapy.

I would also like to mention a person different in every respect—from subjects of interest to character—Jean Piaget, who also suffered from anxiety, neurotic in nature, or as I believe existential, whose mother was mentally ill, and who throughout his life feared madness (Boring & Lindzey, 1952; Fried, 1984).

The above examples illustrate my view about the existence of a myth, generated and nourished by those in power, of a separation between the helper and the being helped, on the one hand, and among helpers themselves, on the other hand. The myth of separatism stems from a collective fear, a collective terror, shared by the human species as a whole, regardless of its members' positions in any hierarchical classification, whether social or professional. Somehow, those who have been empowered to deal with others' fears have become ignorant of their own basic fears. This attitude of separatism embodies far-reaching consequences about the practice of psychotherapy. It separates the therapeutic endeavor from its mutual and egalitarian characteristics intrinsic to the humanization of human suffering.

For the moment let us burden ourselves with an additional question: Is it possible to embody an approach that abolishes separatism and promotes egalitarianism?

CHAPTER TWO

Who Is the Knower? or, the Problem of Mutuality

Let me continue with my heuristic inquiry in an effort to reflect on the nature of the relational encounter between the two parties, the so-called therapist–patient dyad. The reader might need to bear in mind the phenomenon of parallel processes (Kahn, 1979) while we travel through this investigation.

As Whorf (1956) suggests, and as I, at times, definitely agree with the Freudian notion of psychic determinism, I always wondered why the category of "supervision" has been chosen to characterize the nature of this unique relationship. What does this choice imply, and what interpersonal dynamics does it elicit? I could comprehend that the term *supervisor* appropriately and accurately specifies the nature of the relationship in the medical profession, where you must know exactly what tissue you are examining, where it is, and how to remove it; or in the trades such as plumbing, where you have to know exactly how to fuse two copper pipes. In these cases the object is definitive, defined, and concrete. In either case, you can measure the result; it is observable. The terms *supervisor* and *supervisee* in these two instances are justified; one is supervised to perform properly.

However, in the therapeutic setting, I am with you, the so-called client. Nothing about you is concrete, unless I see you through a behaviorist prism, which I do not. Nothing about you is definitive, not even your death, not knowing when, except perhaps your height. I know about you only what you tell me, unless I make you concrete, that is a theoretical unit; then you are a theory but not you. I could wish you not only looked like but actually were a pipe. I could take you, then, "as is" and learn how to fix you if you needed fixing. More than anything I could wish you were a piece of brain tissue; then I could use sophisticated and precise methods of brain surgery, if applicable, or psychological surgery, to teach you that when you think "Y" you should think "X," and that your feelings are just a matter of transportation and duplication—transference, if you prefer.

And when I am with a supervisor, I open by saying that while I am with the other person (the patient or *Other*), I do not understand approximately a third—being very generous to my afflicted ego—of what is happening. Another third I do understand, or think I understand, but for reasons beyond a person's perception—and I am not a mystic—I am not able to convey further, so that I will try my best to convey what little, or much, if you prefer, is left. I was trying to convey a feeling of dignity, respect, and modesty for the parties involved—that little I can do. But the supervisor is not impressed. He pushes forward nonverbally with "let's start working." ("Working," I murmur to myself, what strange wording.) He asks me to introduce myself. I do it willingly, naively convinced that the man sitting across from me is really interested in my professional biography. He is not. How do I know? Well, he is just listening, though attentively, even with empathy, but still silently, never asking, as a matter of politeness or mere curiosity, how "it" was "working" where I was, or with such and such people, or why I moved from one theoretical orientation to another. I am never asked what kind of learning experience I am expecting from this supervisor, what I think would enhance my professional growth and competence, or what is meaningful to me. You might wonder: then what is he, this supervisor, interested in? We are still with the negatives, in accordance with my belief that if we see what therapy is not, then we will have a better knowledge of what it should be. He is not interested in interesting himself to me. He is not interested in letting me get to know him. Who he is, how old he is, where he is from, whether married, divorced, or single, what his learning experience is, what he considers meaningful for therapeutic competence. None of this.

Many sources can be imputed to this attitude on the part of the sometimes therapist and at other times supervisor. The reader might recall the Freudian "opaque mirror," the emotionally aloof, neutral, and nonresponsive analyst, but this attitude certainly is not confined to psychoanalysis, and by itself is not our main concern here. In this matter, schools differ from one another by the degree of anonymity that they allocate to their followers, or at best by the degree of empathy and understanding they express toward the person confronting this anonymity. No school, to my knowledge, debates the anomaly of this anonymity.

It took me a couple of years, chronologically speaking (because to my internal diary it felt like decades), before I found in myself the courage and confidence to dispute my supervisor's supervising position and to label him as a *consultant.* This is not a matter of semantics. I was declaring both a protest and a wish concerning the division of roles for the parties involved, all three of us. I was protesting against the assumptions implicit in the supervising procedure, the focal one being the one that assigns to the expert the role of the knower. The figures on the facing page demonstrate this significant change.

These figures present a shift in hierarchy, in power—no more reliance on an external locus of authority (i.e., on expertism), on any epithets whatsoever, no more impressions, but a real mutual give-and-take interaction. After all, I was sitting with the other person, the so-called client or patient; this was I who "knew" what was going on there, and again I who was going back there to try again to "know" what was going on there. How did I survive this power dynamic? A more relevant question would be how the other party is going to survive—me, as representative of the prospective therapist, included.

I know that at this point your scientific cell is signaling "data validity," "generalizability." Many prospective therapists complain about their training, usually many years later when already established, or when no longer faced with any apparent threat. Few would dare to complain while in the middle of acquiring a license to practice, or while under any other financial, academic, or professional pressure. In her final assignment at the School of Social Work at New York University, Claudia Behr (1994) writes with painful genuineness about her experience as a "lower power person," as a supervisee in an agency "where there is no working as

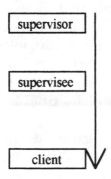

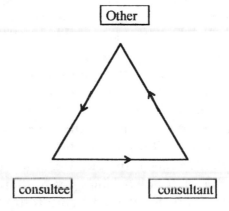

a team such that a feeling of autonomy might be created'' (pp. 7–8). This feeling that each worker has an
equal say in matters, is essential in helping a more
egalitarian structure to form (Patti & Resnick, 1972).
Behr is aware of what Wax (1971) describes as the
necessity to maintain contact with the basic ideologies
and values of the significant other(s) or else we become ''psychological outsiders'' (p. 276). What happens when one's values are in conflict with those of

the significant other(s)? Behr feels that in this case one can only either sacrifice values one is committed to in order to belong, or become a psychological outsider. Naturally, many prefer to comply—too immense is their fear of being an *outcast*—a fear as immensely evident to and in those who consider psychotherapy.

Others have come to know the game and how to play it (Wax, 1971), but the memory of its frustrating and dissatisfying effects is registered for years following the events. In reviewing his own background and personal history, Alexander (1990) does not find any flattering words when he is describing his study of clinical psychology. On the contrary, consolidation of ideas, insights, creativity—all were hampered. His work in assessment, "especially on internship, was mostly involved with answering diagnostic questions with little emphasis on extended discussion of personality dynamics. Therapeutic supervision seemed much more involved with either issues of technique or the *supervisor's* evaluations of my own contributions to the therapeutic mix" (p. 63; emphasis added). In fact, Alexander is complaining about the how of doing psychotherapy, and the well-known transference and countertransference phenomena.

My professional biography reveals unequivocal agreement. As with Alexander, I was interested in studying the verbal data produced by the person in the treatment hour in order to come to formulations about the personality of the person with whom I was working. As usual, I kept bringing to the supervision quite detailed written reports comprising the content of the therapeutic conversation and the nature of the therapeutic interaction. As has been said, wasn't I an ex-historian, and loyal to this tradition, which definitely does not contradict the depth of my loyalty to psychology? Then, like now, I was paying great homage to any primary source. The term *primary source* is borrowed from history and archaeology, denoting that texts have to be understood in the contexts of their conditions of production. The analyst should be concerned with whether a text was written as a result of firsthand experience or from secondary sources, whether it was solicited or unsolicited, edited or unedited, and so on (Webb, Campbell, Schwartz, & Sechrest, 1966).

What is this source saying, and what is the motivation for saying it? What is in the "text," and what is beyond? How can I validate what is in and what is beyond? In other words, who is the interpreter, and what is to be interpreted? While I was struggling—sorry, while I am struggling—with these fundamental questions, the other party, the tertiary source, was beyond any contemplation. Wolberg (1988) says:

> Interestingly, a theoretical system may act as a placebo for the therapist. If there is faith in its verity, the therapist will approach the patient with dogged confidence, and will undoubtedly unearth in the patient the exact constituents that compose his or her theoretical scheme.... The conviction on the part of the patient that the therapist *knows* what is wrong with him or her and has ways that will bring health encourages restoration of mastery. This is irrespective of how valid the therapist's system may be. (p. 28; emphasis added)

Plainly put, the tertiary source, in the supervisory context, or a secondary one, in the therapeutic context, becomes, on behalf of an alleged theoretical system, the primary source; it becomes the *Knower*. In history, when a source claims to be primary, and it is not, they call it forgery. But in psychotherapy, the same reversal is given a scientific seal, "the placebo effect," and is considered essential in "restoration of mastery." But who said therapy is a rational process? Is a rational philosophy (of practice) of therapy possible?

Different therapists use different techniques, or rituals, to convey their sense of mastery. We should remember that any vehicle runs in any direction back and forth, so that the therapist might need, as much as the client, the blessed fruits, as we are told, of a placebo belief in the therapist's belief system. The one I am concerned about, and which runs through almost any theoretical system, and which is in use by any therapist (I almost said: consciously or unconsciously) of whatever theoretical orientation, is the concept of the unconscious.

Before I turn to the next stage, let me pose yet another question: How come so many people, both those who seek help and those who provide help, surrender their autonomy, their recognition of themselves as being the source of knowledge, as being the knower? Later, I will define on the positive side the nature of this knowledge; how this surrender happens, in our case in the therapeutic milieu; and what its individual and social implications are.

CHAPTER THREE

The Unconscious as the Source of Power in Psychotherapy

Zvi Giora (1991), in a beautiful and very intelligent book, says that in any discussion:

> Reason and not authority is the parole of debates and yet, we all know that deeply ingrained beliefs die hard and, in fact, continue to thrive even if convincing arguments are proffered in favor of their discontinuance. . . . The concept of the repressed unconscious and its power for influencing behavior became such a deeply ingrained conviction. . . . Most psychotherapists regard it as a foundation stone, and while any other part of a building may be altered or renewed, foundation stones usually are revered and left untouched. (p. 126)

Why, then, does authority and not reason prevail? Giora leaves the question unanswered. Nevertheless, this resistance to changing a foundation stone merits special treatment. After all, resistance is a phenomenon not confined only to our so-called patient, so why are we lagging behind in our quest for change? My contention with this concept, as with others mentioned in this book, is that we resist change because of its being a power tool in the hands of the user, in the hands of the authority.

Then, as noted before, I was interested in what the "text" says, and equipped with the relevant data, I

stepped into the shrines of "how to do psychotherapy."
But, to my astonishment, I found myself again and again
on the side road. While I was straining to confer with
the other person, the source, the origin of knowledge,
and endeavoring to motivate this person to strain to
glean some sense out of his/her private knowledge—I
was being told by the person in charge (i.e., the supervisor in my case, the therapist in the Other's case), that
I should pay attention to the king's road leading to the
king's palace where dwells the all-mighty highness: the
unconscious. Whose unconscious, one may dare to inquire? Of course, my unconscious and the "patient's."
Who knows what is in there in the unconsciousness? Is
the "patient" the owner? Of course not; the "patient"
is not the expert, no way! If we confer on the Other this
task, we deprive ourselves of our main tool and thus
disable ourselves from making a living. What else is left
for us to do!

The supervision hours went by one after another for
years. I was getting used to the fact, that as the name
implies I was engaged in a very subtle pattern underlying our interpersonal interaction, a pattern I was aware
of and struggled to avoid carrying over to other relationships. Paradoxically, I succeeded in doing psychotherapy thanks to an ability to *unlearn* what I was supposed
to learn. This pattern, mentioned already, though in
different wording, consists of some implicit untold
premises with which the applicant should comply. Every
school has its own premises which are activated the moment the "patient" steps in. I am not referring to technical–procedural requirements, such as responsibility to
keep appointments or bringing material for discussion,
illumination, or analysis, but to a global pattern common to all schools which stems from the inequality of

the relationships, and from conversion of the knower. Let us examine some of the ingredients of this pattern:

You need me. You as patient, student, learner, or supervisee, are under distress or stress, and you need me as an expert. The fact that we—therapists, supervisors, teachers, etc.—need our objects no less, both for our personal well-being and very materially, is concealed not only from them but also from ourselves. At times, many times, the message is boldly present yet unsaid: I am a therapist, I know how the psyche operates, I can manage it, I have been successful in managing it, I am a success, look around, seeing is believing, I am a Ph.D., member of the notable and distinguished Association. . . . (please help yourself).

I would like to remind *ourselves* of the centrality of this little word *need* in a person's existence as a physical and psychological creature. When somebody calls for my services, they are crying for some needs to be met, a very important one of them being a crushed self-image or sense of self-esteem. We do not need a great deal of imagination to understand their intrinsic feelings in front of the notable member of—a member who at times is a "screen on to which the patient can project his *infantile* objects" (A. Reich, 1951; emphasis added), or a warm reflector, to paraphrase a client-centered, pseudo-technical terminology. I will expand on the infantilizing processes in psychotherapy later. However, whatever the nature of this "member," at this moment, one thing is beyond doubt and is highlighted: you need me because you are inflicted with some sort of psychopathology. And this is the last illumination somebody with a crushed self-image "needs."

I know. I have covered this important issue in the previous chapter, and I will deal with it much more throughout the upcoming chapters. We all know that knowledge is power. We all also know that usually power in itself has no value and no meaning unless we give it meaning by using it. This stance of "I know" has a profound impact on the nature and dynamics of therapy.

In a seminar on humanistic–existential psychotherapy, a famous lecturer and writer wrote the word *weather* on the board and asked us to find out its disguised meanings. We tried and tried in vain. The lecturer used this exercise to illustrate "the aggravation the patient feels when somebody out there knows the answer, knows the 'weather.' " This expert's intention was merely to bring to our awareness the experience of the feeling that somebody else knows. Equipped with this knowledge, we would be, the lecturer certainly hoped, more empathic to a patient's feelings—yet another example of the magic of "empathy," in this case being used to circumvent the issue instead of addressing it.

What I claim is that we are both in the same boat, that I do not know either, and that this fact should be conveyed as soon as possible to the other party, hoping this time for his or her empathy, if, as I believe, we strive for:

> the provision of the possibility of a genuine, reliable, understanding, and respecting, caring personal relationship in which a human being whose true self has been crushed by the *manipulative techniques* of those who only wanted to make him "not be a nuisance" to them, can begin at last to feel his own true feelings, and think his own spontaneous thoughts, and find himself to be real. (Guntrip, 1971, p. 182; emphasis added)

The mask of "*I know*," of an expert, of one who knows answers or something that the other does not know, deprives therapy of its true power: the sense of togetherness. In a similar vein, though from a different and more modest point of view, Harry Guntrip (1971) wrote that we cannot "always" know the answers to many questions, "but where patient and therapist are prepared to stick it out *together*, then, at the risk of failure, a profoundly rewarding success can ... be achieved" (p. 196; emphasis added).

Let us examine how some of these manipulative techniques operate, this time within the therapy session. The first one we might call the *manipulation of the unconscious*.

In supervision we were asked again and again to expand on our feelings toward the patient and his or her productions. Gradually I noticed that I was not asked for regular expressions of feelings, but for very specific ones. I came to understand that there are "feelings feelings" and there are countertransference feelings and fantasies. Strange, but at the focus of interest were not my "real" feelings, and even more strange, there came a point that I was not able, according to my supervisor's criterion, to distinguish between the two. If one conceives the therapist as attractive and sexy, it means one is encountering some latent, unknown, inaccessible motifs. In vain, the insistence that one feels a client is attractive and sexy and there is nothing more to it is ignored. But there is and there is; alas one is not conscious about it, the supervisee is told. And this is a real threat to the professional therapeutic image of a budding therapist who is trying to be accepted among the privileged few. To be pointed out implicitly as one who is not in touch with unconscious motivations could be compared to being pointed out as an outcast, an as yet unhealthy prospective member who is in need of psychotherapy or personal analysis. I was wondering about the reasons for this emphasis on my unconscious instead of the patient's, who is the object of the inquiry, until I came to understand that, "The evidence of what is going on in the patient's unconscious, then, is based on an awareness of what is now going on in the analyst's own mind . . . the tool for understanding is the analyst's own unconscious" (A. Reich, 1951, p. 25). The following figure depicts the above flow of the unconscious:

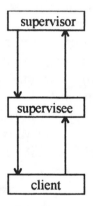

Here we have yet another example of how a text loses its primacy by being replaced by what? In order to know what is going on in the patient's unconscious I have to be aware of my own; in order to do this I have to bring "that" to analysis; in order for the analyst to know what is in my mind and from there to make deductions, interpretations, about the patient's mind—the analyst has to use his or her own "tool," to analyze his or her own unconscious. This is evidence of long-distance manipulation, and this is evidence of what is going on in the supervisor's mind, in a supervisory setting, and in the therapist's mind, in a therapeutic setting. That it is, in fact, what is going on in the patient's mind, it has yet to be demonstrated. But is it important! We know of people who are in good "relationship . . . with [their] own unconscious" (A. Reich, 1951, p. 27) and yet they are miserable and unhappy, unable to make a meaningful change in their life.

Summarizing my experience: I came to know, from a different angle this time, how abusive a reality might become in terms of restricting my autonomy and bending it toward a set of scientific creeds on which, being a scientist, I had full intentions of casting doubt. I'll never forget the fears of being "outcast," of being accused as: one who is in conflict with his unconscious (i.e., with his id, with his impulses, he is immature, over-independent), the spectrum of titles as wide as you can imagine.

Another manipulative technique—and right away I would like to propose that any technique by definition is manipulative in nature—is *manipulation of the relationship*. This sort of manipulation has many facets; some operate under the guise of a well-rationalized technique, some operate by producing and maintaining a professional myth, and still others operate by utilizing both conditions. We have come to a point where, "Virtually anything anyone might do in the company of another person may now be defined as psychotherapeutic. If the definer has the proper credentials, and if the audience is sufficiently gullible, any such act will be publicly accepted and accredited as a form of psychotherapy" (Szasz, 1978, p. xii). How frightening a reality! All you need is a symbol, preferably but not necessarily containing the combination p-h-d, which you may attain first by depleting your own and your parents' savings;

then by demonstrating good enough memorizing capabilities in choosing the best possibility out of four unknowns; then by being smart and picking up a subject for research that is as remote as possible from your very core of interests ("You do want to finish it, don't you?"). The research should of course be within the particular range of interests (i.e., prevailing wisdom), of that particular institution, which wants to enlarge the "body of human knowledge" but certainly its own body too. And we wonder why so few are soulful and so many are poor architects. Now all you need is a group of adherents, and you are on your way to establishing your own cult—of psychotherapy.

Szasz forgets that in the beginning we were all naive and that the gullibles of today are a by-product of a coercive reality he so eloquently undertakes to abolish. Some crash under the eminent and incomprehensible power of hypocrisy and pretense, that confusing gap between what we say we are doing and what we actually do.

Hodder (1994) points out that a full sociological analysis cannot be restricted to interview data, because "what people say" is often very different from "what people do" (p. 395). The author contends that we must also consider material traces. Szasz (1968) emphasizes the importance of studying what therapists are doing rather than what they say they are doing, "a point," the editors comment, "which no one would seriously dispute" (p. 241). Analysis of a live recording of a session might be considered as a material trace, in contrast to clinical cases reproduced in textbooks and articles, and might help in minimizing the above gap.

One person did not crash under the interplay between self and persona. They were one in him. Actually he did what he said he was doing, and he was praised by the most eminent figures in psychotherapy. I came to know his "technique" in the introductory course of my second year of graduate studies. My professor, a good architect of soul indeed, played back for us an audio cassette of a session in which John Rosen, who includes himself as one of the "innovators," treats Jim. Poor Jim, I should say. On that day my naiveté absorbed a painful blow. I believed that by turning to psychology I was going to encounter a humane and compassionate way of dealing with other human beings. The word *psychology* was wrapped with a charm of humanism, understanding, delicacy, and grace. The evils of this invalid creature are well known today (Masson, 1988), and by themselves are not our concern here. Then, backed by positive references from no less than Donald Winnicott, Carl Rogers, Harold Searles, Frieda Fromm-Reichmann, Michael Balint, Ronald Fairbairn, and more (Masson, 1988), this man by his doings was *the* materialization of my darkest dreams. I was not gullible; I understood that there was a crack in the mental health profession.

In Rosen's work, the above techniques of manipulation of the unconscious, relationship, expertism, and technique mingle together extremely well. Under the guise of his greater knowledge, he assumes the role of the knower, usurps control over a citizen claiming he knows the content of his unconscious, therefore his needs, "invents" a strategy, a technique, using a prevailing ill-defined wisdom, and boldly, yet with scientific articulation, *abuses* a person in a relationship for his own good. The tragedy is that nobody, again, *nobody* protests! Eventually he is stopped when, as Masson (1988) puts it, "a number of Rosen's patients had had enough abuse, and determined to come forward and to seek justice" (p. 166).

Establishments are always late following after events, and this is true not only in Rosen's case. The motivation for systematic, large-scale investigation of the long-term psychological effects of combat came not from the military or the medical establishment, but from the organized efforts of soldiers themselves. Women organized outside the framework of medicine or the mental health system, and brought about the same social response to victims of rape and domestic violence (on both cases see Herman, 1992).

How is it that somebody can scientifically exert power for the sake of power, personal power, and is not stopped by the scientific establishment? Well, as already said, there is no course offered anywhere in the world on the power structure of psychotherapy. Why the ignorance, you ask? What might happen if in debating power issues profoundly and honestly we come to acknowledge that psychotherapy as defined today is a myth, that we invent techniques because of our own shortcomings, and not because there is, in reality, any need for them? But we are scrupulous professionals, and we do not want to desert a no-man's land. We are great as inventors—our material being manipulation of words, concepts, and terms. We invent a superimposed structure, name it, and believe that we also address this issue. Later we will examine the uses and misuses of transference and countertransference. Now, let us go back to Rosen, who I believe demonstrates how the atypical has become typical.

Rosen (1969) begins with a brief review of Jim's mental status and history, which is full of implied meanings.

The listeners are to understand that Jim's acute paranoid episode "rapidly subsided" thanks to the merits of direct analysis, and that Jim's reluctance to return to "the prescribed continuing therapy for the neoneurosis which followed the resolution of the psychosis" [note the use of language] is responsible for his relapse. Rosen wants us also to believe that Jim remained well for about a year, again due to the impact of his method, but you are free to deduce that it happened due to its absence. In fact, the introductory passage is so laden with manipulative statements that it is impossible to tap into the truth. We are also led to believe that Jim willingly and purposefully asked for this specific treatment, again thanks to its benign effects. You see, he liked it! Anyway, we know that at the moment of the current recording Jim was in therapy "on and off for eight months," and that he is in a straitjacket.

R.: *Why are you in a straitjacket? Don't shake your head* [he commands], *answer me! . . . Do you understand that?* [He almost shouts at Jim.]

J.: *I don't know.*

Remember, Jim is not a criminal, and this passage, the beginning one, is supposed to exemplify a method of therapy and not interrogation. As a matter of fact, it seems that nowadays you can interrogate a helpless and confined person who is labeled "mad" and call it some sort of *analysis*, which sounds much more sophisticated than mere *therapy*, a general term. But the human spirit, in whom it exists, does not distinguish between a mad spirit and Ph.D./M.D. spirit. Though confined, Jim *resists* this crude exercise of power.

Rosen continues: he presses Jim to admit that he was going to kill himself, and he does that by putting Jim down, treating him as a stupid child, *infantilizing* him. He goes around and around squeezing Jim while what he is asking could be done so simply as, for example: "Jim, I want to make sure you understand why you are in a straitjacket. It is because we believe that by holding that nail in the bathroom you intended to kill yourself." *Simplification,* by which I mean making the therapy process "simple but not simpler," would be another object of my approach. In this statement, we give Jim his very basic rights as a human being living in a democratic society and protected by it: the benefit of the doubt. But Rosen assumes that he is the one who knows, he is the source of knowledge; and in vain are Jim's protests that he wasn't going to kill himself. In fact, we have very good reasons to be tempted to withdraw the benefit of doubt from Rosen: Why is Jim really in a straitjacket? Could it be for the sake of the demonstration? The explanations are very vague and not convincing—he was caught in the bathroom with a nail in his hand. Is this a sufficient reason to confine somebody? Of course Rosen knows that it is not, so he relies on Jim's past history, knowing that he cut his wrist twice, once with a razor and another time with a piece of glass, and knowing that "he had been talking about killing himself, about dying," they decided to take no chances, and confined him.

With professional and credentialed manipulators one cannot sort out truth from fiction, unless one listens very carefully to every sentence and every intonation, and then one encounters the morbid superficiality. For this educated person, killing yourself and dying are equivalent! Not so for the so-called "insane" person, Jim. He, as well as we, knows that one might have thoughts about death and dying without any intention to killing oneself even though he once did have such an intention and even once acted upon it in the past. But for the one-dimensional personality life proceeds in a linear manner (Marcuse, 1964)—life as well as personal relationships, which are characterized by hierarchy and exploitation of the subordinates. Here we are concerned with a very specific manifestation of power exerted in a unique and very specific setting which by its very nature is prone to the exploitation of power, and which paradoxically is not being addressed either by the scientific community or by the public. I am talking about kinds of power abuse which cannot be addressed legally, nor they can be inserted into a code of ethics. It entails a systemic approach, and it can be abolished only when it becomes apolitical.

Rosen, politically legitimized, continues his maneuvers with a person who is considered and named, by the same political system as not being in touch with reason, and therefore is placed under the guardianship of a person with reason. In listening to this recording one doubts which party, at least at that point in time, maintains reason. Now, observe the intensity and severity of the helplessness felt by one cast out as insane in the face of constitutional and methodological power abuse:

Rosen wants to be reassured that Jim understands his explanation of the reasons for his confinement. The separatist therapist is not interested in mutual agreement. Accordingly, Rosen continues:

R.:   . . . *Do you understand that?* [He almost shouts at Jim.]

J.:   *Yes, sir.* [with subjection]

R.:   *What did I just say?* [We don't know how old Jim is; he certainly is not a child; however, I believe that even a child should not be infantalized.]

Long pause. [It seems nothing is evolving. Things have been explained and approval has been guaranteed; what else is left? Count on the knower]:

R.:   *Look at me* [he orders]; *as you sit here thinking now, are you thinking that you would not like to kill yourself?* [He rebukes Jim]: *When you shake your head the microphone can't hear it.*

[Rosen is not interested in what Jim is really thinking about. Maybe he is protecting himself by projecting onto Jim his own wishful thoughts, coercing him to believe in them. It might very well be that Jim would actually *like* literally to kill himself at that very moment. How would you feel being tied up in a straitjacket, degraded into the ground by being whipped up mercilessly with pseudo-wise words?]

Silence. Jim apparently smiles [at times this is what is left in the face of absurdity]:

R.:   *I see you are still able to smile, anyway* [laughs].

J.:   *I don't know how.*

R.:   *Hm!*

J.:   *I don't know how and why.*

R.:   *Why what?* [Rosen apparently does not understand what is going on. It was not included in his preplanned program. For the separatist therapist there is no room for spontaneity and novelty by anybody else. Jim explains it to the man of reason]:

J.:   *I am still able to smile.* [One really wonders, but not Rosen]:

R.:   *Why do you say that with such a forlorn . . . for-*
        lorn . . . why is that your hopeless point of view, you
        can't understand why you are able to smile at all any-
        more. What is happening to you that is so terrible?
        [Of course, it is a misperception of Jim's reality.
        He did not say he is unable to smile "at all any-
        more," but we should not underestimate Jim, as
        does this so-called therapist, and allow him to
        plead his case about why he *did* smile.]

J.:   [Long pause] *What's so terrible that is* [long pause]
        losing feelings, probably, that is what is so terrible
        in that.

R.:   [Impatiently]: *Explain that to me. It is a little diffi-*
        cult to understand [!]. *You losing feeling about what?*

J.:   *About even being alive.*

R.:   *You losing feeling about even being alive as though*
        you don't care whether being alive or not. [The sepa-
        ratist does not ask the source of knowledge for
        interpretations. He gives them, misplacing him-
        self as the knower.]

J.:   [Decisively]: *No, it is not like that.*

R.:   [Impatiently]: *What is it? I don't understand you.*

Long pause.

J.:   *When you talk to a person and keep talking to him and*
        he still doesn't understand . . . it . . . I just don't get
        it, if it's been so long a person should understand some-
        thing. . . .

Jim bravely resists. This resistance is different from
those the scientific literature talks about abundantly.
Jim is not resisting the therapist's interpretations per se
aimed at repressed unconscious wishes and conflicts,
as psychoanalysis claims (Fenichel, 1934; Freud, 1926/
1959). Neither does he resist because he wants to avoid

"being truly subjectively present . . . in the therapeutic work," due to a pending threat to his familiar identity, as some humanistic approaches claim (Bugental, 1987, p. 175). Jim is truly subjectively present. Both theories' basic tenet is that resistance essentially is unrealistic, and is aimed at preventing the constructive forces from manifesting themselves and leading toward mental health. The therapist is taught to watch out for and handle these self-defeating tendencies whenever they arise. The patient, we are told, is not resisting the personality of the therapist, who the therapist is, and what the therapist is doing de facto, but either transferring and projecting onto the therapist image a remote figure, say father or mother or any significant other in the life of the patient, as if the therapist's figure, hopefully not a remote one, is not a significant other by itself; or the therapist is fearful of an abstract yet still remote threat to his or her existence. In these formulations, in my opinion, hide the seeds of great and unprecedented tribulation. What if there is a real and not remote threat to one's existence? What if that threat derives from the person of the therapist? He. She. What he is. What she is. How is one going to protect oneself? The therapist is not abusing me physically; I can't even say he or she is abusing me psychologically. How can I accuse a system, a methodology? If I comply, I betray my feelings, the very reason why I came to psychotherapy in the first place, and if I don't, I risk being cast out as oppositional, as having difficulties with authority, as being nontreatable—you name it. Maybe I should rise up and leave; at least I have this privilege, even if I am not sure I have the privilege of possessing enough courage to "act out." Then, maybe my feelings betray me! Oh, I had an insight! The therapist was right, competently right. This is my father. No. Mother. Both. None of them. Even not the therapist. It is *me*.

Later I will debate the erroneous notion of "What is outside is inside." In the meantime let us remember that Jim is still resisting the power structure of psychotherapy. He resists erroneous interpretations, faked expertism, and power plays. He exemplifies my notion that whenever there is a display of resistance in therapy, it should be given due realistic respect. In other words, the possibility that the other person is reacting to an implicit yet actual power component present in the meeting, in the therapist's personality or in both—this component should be given first priority. Upon its mutual resolution, both parties may move on into other sources which impede the ongoing process.

The fate of Jim's heroic resistance illuminates what often happens in these cases, and how the power component inherent in psychotherapy, together with the power assigned to the pathographizer and withheld from the pathographized, perpetuate a human predicament—that of abuse.

Going back to poor Jim, let us remember also that his mood—"forlorn"—*is* congruent, using professional clinical terminology, with what he says and above all with his immediate reality. His reality testing and judgment are intact. He is sane in an insane situation. Do you wonder what would have happened if Jim had addressed the chief medical director complaining he had been manipulated, misunderstood, ridiculed, infantalized, degraded, and provoked? He would have listened to Jim empathically, nodding his head with comprehension, making sure Jim was not upset anymore, and would have dismissed him from the room. Then he would have opened Jim's chart and noted beside the date: "Ideas of reference, this time toward Dr. Rosen." Who would believe a paranoid? How can he believe himself when his very real feelings and accurate perceptions are denied existence:

R.:   *Yes, now, who doesn't understand, you or I* [pause]
       by that I mean, are you trying to tell me something
       that I don't get or are you disturbed because I am trying
       to tell you something that you don't get? [a very clear
       manipulation "inviting" Jim to comply with the
       authority]
J.:   *Well, I think it's both.*

In the remaining time, Rosen continues to behave in accordance with the patterns we discussed above. Jim is lowered to dirt and dust. At one point Rosen applies his "direct analysis" which is nothing more than the age old practice known in our profession as the "technique" of confrontation. It is the same phenomenon under a different name, and Rosen is cited by himself, and by respectable others, as being among the "innovators." Of course, Rosen applies his own flavor of crude distaste: He says he knows, what else, what Jim is looking for, and here comes the great revelation—Jim needs to be "attached to *something*," because, Rosen keeps on analyzing:

> *You never had the love of a mother* [in Rosen's healthy
> mentality a mother is something, not someone];
> *she couldn't be attached to you; you tried to be attached*
> *to her, but you know she called up here and said she had*
> *hoped you would be dead. . . . You know that she has*
> *been institutionalized, look at me! You know she has*
> *been mentally sick, don't you? Don't shake your head,*

say yes or no! . . . *And when a person is mentally sick they can't be concerned about somebody else, they are too busy being concerned about themselves. We call that narcissism, if you like. Do you understand that? The way you get upset can you be worrying about somebody else?* [Of course Jim agrees that he is not, and he understands that the latest lab exam shows traces of another chronic virus they, the experts, call . . . something with . . . *ism*; it harms your capacity for, I didn't quite understand whether concern or worry or both. The Doc mentioned both.] . . . *So you'll never be able to find your mother, then you're trying to find your father, but he was very unresponsive* [now he demolishes the father, and in a moment you will understand why]. . . . *You are trying to find peace someplace; you're trying to find some kind of unity for yourself* . . . [Jim is accused of not finding that peace and unity in that place with Dr. Rosen, for surely it is not Dr. Rosen's fault, because obviously he can relate to everybody in that place. Slowly he leads the way for Jim to understand that it is because something, another thing, is wrong with him that he is not able to relate to Dr. Rosen.] . . . *Why don't you love me?* . . . *Why don't you get up and put your arms around me and give me a kiss?* . . . [a therapist may be so much invested in one's theoretical schemes and maneuvers that one's eyes betray even the physical reality of a real person. Jim is still in the straightjacket. Yet, if one imagines what could have happened to Jim if he was not protected by the straightjacket, then one could tragically say how fortunate Jim was!] . . . *You don't want to come near me.* . . . *Are you afraid that it would mean something homosexual if you did that?* . . . [The rest comprises Dr. Rosen's wisdom on matters of love, sex, the penis, "every man has unconscious homosexuality"; two minds in a person one conscious and the other, the intelligent one, the unconscious. . . .]

We all know the Freudian theory concerning unconscious homosexuality as the cause of delusional disorders. Less known is *how* Freud arrived at his theories. He read Schreber's autobiography, *Memoirs of My Nervous Illness*, never having met him in person, but theorizing from his review of the autobiography (Kaplan & Sadock, 1991). Again, if one has access to the between-the-lines, to the unconscious, then one does not need personal verification; one does not need *the* person. One can even use a secondary source and arrive at hypotheses that are not at most a brilliant piece of literature, if you wish, but a science applicable to the habitants of the Western hemisphere. There is no need of the source itself, the *primary* one. Like father, like son, Rosen keeps the tradition alive. He knows the content of the person's unconscious; and has no need of Jim for verification of validity. If Jim resists, he is in denial, and in need of more analysis. So powerful is the impact of a forefather that new and compelling evidence to the contrary falls on deaf ears. (Clinical evidence has not supported Freud's thesis. A significant number of delusional patients do not have demonstrable homosexual tendencies, and the majority of homosexual men do not have symptoms of paranoia or delusions [Kaplan & Sadock, 1991]).

Is Rosen an exception? I believe he is a mirror reflecting how therapists can harm their so-called patients under the guise of their alleged greater wisdom. Rosen definitely utilized heavy dosages of what I have summed up in the phrase *Power Structure of Psychotherapy.* Yet, I

remind the reader, that Rosen was praised by very notable psychotherapists, and that he would not have been
able to perform his power plays without official approval
of his (pseudo-)scientific methods. Is Rosen's spirit
alone in the world of psychotherapy? Is it confined to
the so-called psychotics?

Miller and Rollnick (1991) venture to understand
how we, as professional counselors, can facilitate and
motivate change while working with addictive behaviors.
They launch into the problem by first asking, "Where
did we go wrong?" (p. 5), and what they consequently
describe is an unequivocal demonstration of the power
structure of psychotherapy, and its potentials for abuse.

The prominent mechanism by which, this time,
abuse was implemented is the tactic of confrontation.
It warrants quoting a sample from the lips of Chuck
Dederich, founder of Synanon, to a Mexican-Ameri-
can addict:

> Now, Buster, I'm going to tell you what to do. And I'll
> show you. You either do it or you'll get the hell off Syna-
> non property. You shave off the mustache, you attend
> groups, and you behave as a gentleman as long you live
> here. You don't like it here? God bless you, I'll give you
> the same good wishes that I gave other people like you
> when they left and went off to jail. That's the way we
> operate in Synanon; you see, you are getting a little emo-
> tional surgery. If you don't like the surgery, fine, go and
> do what you have to. Maybe we'll get you again after you
> get out of the penitentiary or after you get a drug over-
> dose. "Nobody tells me what to do!" Nobody in the world
> says that except dingbats like dope fiends, alcoholics, and
> brush-face-covered El Gatos. (p. 6)

Extracting from this extreme, shivering yet real example, and other cases, the authors remonstrate:

How did we come to believe that a certain class of human beings is possessed of a unique condition that requires us to use aggressive confrontation if we wish to help them? How did it become believable, justifiable, and acceptable to rely upon such hostile tactics for addressing certain addictive behaviors, when these same approaches would be seen as reflecting at best poor judgment (if not malpractice) in treating most other psychological and medical problems? (Miller & Rollnick, 1991, p. 7)

How really? Let us listen to what Miller and Rollnick (1991) have to say:

A key assumption underlying aggressive confrontational strategies is that alcoholics (drug addicts, offenders, etc.)—*as a class*, as an inherent part of their condition—possess extraordinary high levels of certain defense mechanisms . . . that these are deeply ingrained in such individuals' personality and character. . . . They appear to have arisen gradually *in practice*, guided in part by the vaguely psychodynamic belief that alcoholics and others with drug problems are characterized by "an addictive personality" or unusually "strong defenses." (pp. 8–9)

No doubt, the authors' ideas and approach represent a revolution in the politics of therapy. Because of the belief that "you can't reason with them," with alcoholics, no one thought of applying or teaching Rogerian principles with alcoholics. Nevertheless, it is a limited, though very welcome, revolution. It is my contention that the authors' formulations contain an internal contradiction, of which the authors themselves might have been aware and which, at any rate, should be scrutinized in order to bring their ideas to their ultimate conclusion.

The authors actually espouse the very basics they disapprove of. They nullify the importance of technique, or specifics, in precipitating change. But these enter the stage from the back door, this time under a different name: strategy. These strategies are intended to help one "not assume an authoritarian role." The authors actually point at us—psychologists, psychotherapists, health professionals of all kinds—as the source of the ineffectiveness of our therapeutic efforts with addicts. We are ineffective because we apply theoretical concepts—confrontation. We misunderstand human psychology and the meaning of ambivalence, and we use wrong, power-oriented techniques derived out of misconception and misunderstanding. So, herein lies the shortcoming, which to my understanding highlights my line of argument that even in this refreshing formulation of therapy, the change that is being advocated is a matter of form and not substance. The question is very important, and the authors do not address it: why only with addicts? The problem of stigmatization is shared by all who are labeled and pathogenized; all, and not only alcoholics, are treated *"as a class"* with corresponding psychological defense characteristics (such as splitting with borderline, repression with hysteria, reaction formation with obsessive-compulsion, etc. Denial is characteristic of all though it is attributed "strongly" to addicts); all, and not only alcoholics, are susceptible to threats to their freedom by submitting to psychotherapy.

Addictions comprise a host of various mental nosologies such as alcohol and other drug abuse, eating disorders, pathological gambling, and other compulsions. Addictive behaviors and neuroses, as well as disorders of personality, share several central characteristics such as self-defeating behavior, pursuit of instant short-term gratification, problems with self-esteem and self-assertion, etc. Why are the principles underlying "motivational interviewing" not recommended as applicable also with others? These principles are so universal, so essential in any human interaction, especially in person-to-person interaction, that their confinement to a section (or a class) of the population deprives them of meaning unless we treat them as a *set of strategies*. In conclusion, the reader still encounters the very questions the authors ventured to address, because we get a replacement of one concept with another—technique with strategy—and a second replacement of one class with another.

On page 12 the authors relate again to their basic assumption backed by research that "the denial hypothesis—that alcoholics or 'chemically dependent' people *'as a class'* evidence particular personality abnormalities or unusually high levels of certain defenses—is a *Myth*" (emphasis added). Here, it seems to me, lies the reason, or should we say the fear—behind the confinement mentioned above—because if we ask why we do not extend this argument to other realms of mental suffering, and we can easily back up any argument with contradictory research findings, then we are in proximity with the myth of mental illness.

Of course, as the authors would certainly agree, we are not supposed to resort to coercive authoritarian practices in cases where an alcoholic, *as an individual,* evidences unusually high levels of certain defenses. Reliance on such practices is *not* a function of the object, the person patient, but of the person therapist and a scientific lore which adheres to separatist worldviews and claims of being the knower. (To learn about what goes wrong, in terms of power abuse, with other people when we treat them as "classes," and in this case as victims of human-made [of double meaning] trauma— war and sexual abuse—see Herman, 1992.)

Let me now examine some dimensions of power exertion in psychotherapy, of personality disorders from a different, much praised and popular angle: that of "cognitive therapy."

CHAPTER FOUR

"Cognitions" as a Source of Power in Psychotherapy

A long time ago I wanted to acquaint myself with Beck's system of psychotherapy, so I set out to study this emerging field in psychology and psychotherapy which some call the "cognitive revolution" (Howard, 1991). I saw Carl Rogers, Fritz Perls, and Albert Ellis interview Gloria in *Three Approaches to Psychotherapy* (Shostrom, 1965). And I loved—*Gloria*. She was articulate, intelligent, sensitive, with an air of contagious openness. Gloria herself provided the best testimony to what really happened: She was deeply touched by Rogers' attitude toward her, and until her death some 15 years later, she wrote to Rogers a couple of times a year. The film provided both of them with a deeply shared common experience. As Rogers said in reference to their 30-minute filmed interview: "It is good to know that even one half-hour can make a difference in a life" (quoted in Weinrach, 1990, p. 287). As for her encounter with Perls, she felt he tried to dominate her. He obviously was trying to exert an expert's power on her during the filmed interview, and, as we learn, also afterwards. Albert Ellis, on the other hand, was, well, a thinking system, geared toward her brain, her distorted belief system, and not capable of any empathic listening. Gloria did not have much to say about this interview with Ellis. Neither he nor his RET left any significant impression on her life. I can say the same for my professional life. I never underestimated the importance of a person's belief system, thoughts, imagination, inherited storied beliefs, or learned beliefs. Yet, in psychotherapy I equate cognition with meaning—a piece of cognition or a belief representing an effort by the person to deliver a message to him/herself, to me, to us in the broad sense.

Now we are at the end of the second millenium C.E., and I would like to share with the reader a systematic encounter with cognitive therapy. I will cite a few well-circulated books on the subject and a careful listening to a recording of Beck doing cognitive psychotherapy of "an avoidant personality disorder" (Beck, 1990). You will understand then why I was reminiscing about the 1980s and Gloria.

I read a lot. It is a habit, a beloved one, yet not one that is interchangeable with experience. I have always had that urge to look behind the letters to find the human being who is holding that pen that produces those worlds with words. But reading alone does not provide the kind of holistic intellectual satisfaction I yearn for. And actually, that is why I am involved in the applied science of psychology. I need a personal, person-to-person, encounter. This urge is exceptionally intense when I am encountering a professional issue. I always welcome an in vivo reproduction as an adjunct to the mute words—especially in our profession where there are gaps all around, as I have emphasized throughout my current writing. Such devices as audio- or video-cassettes, render an authentic, direct account of the events which is less contaminated by intellectual and other disguises than the written word.

In this set of cassettes, Beck ventures to demonstrate that cognitive therapy is effective not only with depressive patients but also with patients suffering from personality disorders. From the beginning you come to learn the elasticity of these nosological concepts. It is amazing how some clinicians play around with their own self-invented concepts and entities:

> B (Beck): The patient whose interview you will be hearing shortly had been in treatment with Dr. Susan Byers. She had originally been diagnosed as having a generalized anxiety disorder and major depressive disorder. In addition she had an axis II diagnosis of mixed personality disorder with prominent avoidant features. Since avoidance was the most prominent aspect of her difficulties at the time of my interviews with her, I chose to focus on that problem area.

Beck's patient, Audrey, and Gloria have much more in common than their gender. Both are extremely intelligent, articulate, open, and sensitive. And both, for this purpose, were interviewed by male therapists. I would not have dwelt on this important fact at present but I feel I am compelled to, because, a few moments after the above diagnostic passage, and after a thorough description of the dynamics of avoidant personality disorder, we learn that "a series of unpleasant events precipitated the generalized anxiety disorder and major depressive disorder. One of these *unpleasant* [!] experiences, in fact a very severely unpleasant experience, had been the experience of being raped sometime prior to her first being seen at our center."

Please pause. . . .

Do you notice the abuse cycle?

This woman has been through a terror (not merely "unpleasant" and not "one of a series of events," but a major event). Rape is abuse of power or, correctly put, abuse of lack of power of the victim. Of course, it is only natural that such a victimized person would feel general anxiety and overwhelming depression. It is normal. Wouldn't you, if you had been raped and/or sod-omized? What is not natural is the way in which she has been raped again. She has been deprived of her normality by being labeled as sick in the face of an ab-normal event. The pathographizing process does not know mercy. We are to understand that the "real" pre-cipitating factor to her current ailment is not the rape itself, the trauma, but her underlying personality struc-ture. Once again we see the importance of the question of etiology. It is of fundamental importance because it dictates the therapist's personal and professional atti-tude toward that person. For example, for Beck, Audrey is a "patient," as he persistently calls her, because she is sick, her personality being inherently defective prior to the rape. The rape just serves as a trigger; while for someone else she is a tragic victim of a private form of organized social violence (see Herman, 1992, p. 61), who acknowledges the ancillary contribution of "pre-morbid personality" but knows that "with severe enough traumatic exposure *no person* is immune" (p. 57; emphasis added). It is not—or not only—a question of morality (psychotherapy and ethics being insepara-ble). As we will see, one's point of view dictates one's professional therapeutic approach, and leads in many cases to the perpetuation of the abuse cycle.

Beck says, and wants us to believe, that Audrey "had for the most part worked through the impact of this very traumatic event with the help of Dr. Byers," so that now the time is ripe for an encounter, a very specific encounter, with the main dish, the very core of her misery: "the basic structure of her personality disor-der." Surprisingly, Beck is as oblivious to the host of research findings about the prolonged recovery of rape victims (Herman, 1992; Kirschner & Kirschner, 1993; Russell, 1986; Sadock, 1989), as he is to the obvious trauma of the rape. That is what happens when one needs and addresses a category, not a person, and when one needs a "proof" of the efficiency of a technique.

A few seconds before the interview begins, Beck describes Audrey's key distorted basic beliefs that can open the window to her difficulties. He believes that:

> Audrey interprets other people's conversations with her as felt with criticism. In actuality, many of the questions that other people ask her may simply be neutral inquiries or even attempts to build a bridge with her. However, Audrey's views of these interchanges are distorted through the lens of her belief system. More specifically, the concept "Others view me as an object" shapes her interpretation of others behaviors.

What we notice here is that we have an expert on—reality, "actuality," in his own words. What Audrey *believes* is the reality, her personal subjective reality is called distortion. What that expert *believes* is the reality is presumed to be factual! Why this partial, unequal attitude? Psychotherapy is not an egalitarian endeavor. In a separatist system there is always one who is being put down and labeled as inferior, sick, the "patient" one who has to adjust his or her perception of reality to that of the dominant other in order to hold in fact an illusion that he or she is getting out of the inferior position and approaching the preferred one. We do remember the fear of ostracism, don't we? I will demonstrate in a moment the inevitable hazards (i.e., distortions) of such a situation: the scientist-therapist is the one who is distorting, at the very least, the nature of the interaction—and this is the only reality that counts because

Audrey's past history is only an approximation of that reality—and the so-called "patient" is the one who holds a firm and accurate grasp of her own reality. She is being really used, and "viewed as an object." And we will see what happens when one is not aware of and sensitive to the kind of resistance that stems from a therapist's abuse of power.

The Interviews

The First Session

Audrey starts by relating that recently she has been going through another pretty strong wave of anxiety, which she had been having periodically for quite some time. She relates it to her job: "I work in a job where I have been sexually harassed, where I have received a lot of racially unkind comments." She feels unappreciated at work, and relates that when on a trip outside the country she encountered, once again, a situation with some of the people she was traveling with which she felt very annoying: She noticed that when she was present, all of a sudden the topic of the conversation would take a turn.

Audrey, as in the case of many people in such situations, starts the session by giving several "reasons" why she feels the way she feels: (1) anxiety, (2) sexual harassment, (3) racial intimidation, (4) a trip. And a therapist is confronted with the task of choosing which issue to follow up. But is this the task of the therapist? Is the therapist the one who should make the choice? We have three choices: to let the other person make the choice; to assign that role to the therapist; or to assign the task to mutual exploration. Of course, an egalitarian, person-to-person oriented, conversational therapy would choose the third choice, yet it is considered legitimate, at least in the scientific literature, to go for the second, "expert" alternative. According to Beck's "expert" oriented system, this is the therapist who formulates a therapy plan for each session, establishes an agenda at the beginning of the session, and formulates and tests concrete hypotheses. (Beck, Rush, Shaw, Emery, 1979, pp. 75–78). And Beck makes the choice for Audrey—and instead of her. Do you know why? Because he believes that *he knows*, that he is *the knower*. The consequences of this attitude are quite tragic in that they perpetuate the abuse cycle by imposing on the other person a set of underlying assumptions (i.e., a theory, a set of beliefs) and treating the other person as sick, maladjusted, irrational, disoriented to real reality but relating to a twisted internal "reality." In other words, the individual is being objectified. And that is exactly what happens to Audrey.

Cognitive technology is geared toward "specificity" because only then can it muster a specific preplanned "strategy." By its nature, technology can deal only with specific units, or short units, in contrast to the "long units" of Murray (1938, p. 39). Therefore, it is only natural (on behalf of the technology of course) to pick up on a specific *situation* of the trip, and try to analyze it in order to identify and correct, as the technology dictates, the specific logical errors in the patient's thinking (Beck et al., 1979). Beck immediately falls on this opportunity and asks Audrey: "Now Audrey, at the time the conversation took that turn what . . . what did you feel then?"

But Beck's inquiry leads to the third "reason" Audrey stated as responsible for her recurring anxiety. Once again, we do not have any choice but to go with the person. Audrey says, with a trembling voice, that she had been mistreated in her own family, and that as time went on she came to realize that there were differences in her family on the basis of skin color, and because she happened to be of a darker complexion she was basically treated more or less as a servant to her family, with the role of having to do things or clean things. You would agree, I guess, that this is a touching testimony. Now listen to Beck's response: "Can you remember any particular incident that stands out in your mind regarding being treated as a servant?"

The lack of empathy is egregious. Beck basically does not believe her. As the technology deems, Audrey is a victim not of real intrafamilial racism but of cognitive distortions due to either one or a combination of the following: personalization, jumping to conclusions, overgeneralization (Burns, 1980). Again, an expert believes he has the power to question the validity of another's reality. She is sick, right? Can you also see the importance of the issue of etiology? Cognitive theory assumes that it is the person's cognitions (versus fantasies as in psychoanalytic theory) that are responsible for emotional suffering. Once again, though from a different avenue, we learn that "what is inside is outside." And we have another "adjustment theory" which transfers the source of psychopathology from society to the individual. We do not know how accurate Audrey's perception of her familial racial affiliations is, yet we do not have any reason to doubt her perception unless we are caught in the self-fulfilling cycle of the pathographizing phenomenon.

Audrey recalls that at dinner her sister was allowed to talk, but she was not. She insists, backing herself up with plenty of evidence, that her sense of her remote reality is intact and accurate. Beck had to give up this line of inquiry. But I ask you to pay attention to what this woman is saying: *I did not have a say.* I will elaborate later on this central theme in her life as represented in genuine life experience history.

At this point Audrey is being asked, "So, in a nutshell, what do you think was the impact of the early experiences within your family on the way you view yourself now and the way you think others view you?" Again, listen carefully to what this articulate woman has to say: she came to realize, "In many cases, no matter what I really say, what I really do, or what I really achieve, there are some individuals who have really fixed viewpoints about who you are, how you are supposed to be, and how you are supposed to act, and I feel virtually powerless to do anything about that, so I do feel bad . . . [interrupted by Beck]." Who is she talking about? Which cases?

Beck is not attentive to any interpersonal cues. He is cued only toward those malfunctioning belief systems of mental filtering, magnification, overgeneralization, and so on. He wants to assure her that there were other instances where she had been treated as a real person, and there were indeed, as she does assure him; and then he proceeds with the technical routine of "It sounds like you have a couple of beliefs in there . . . " and he summarizes her beliefs, falling far short of Audrey's own account. Once again the conversation that evolves touches Audrey's main concern to which Beck is oblivious: she resents being patronized, that her points of view are discarded, and that she was not, in a particular case, even considered to be a thoughtful person. She feels that certain people use her because she is capable of doing certain things, and when they reach their goal they say "Good-bye, Audrey." And she goes back to talk about the first "reason" for her emotional distress, her anxiety, which she relates to her difficulty in being assertive with individuals "that will either come down hard on me or they will ignore me; or if I say something, I will feel even worse than I did in the first place."

At this point it becomes obvious that there exists another layer of events. Audrey becomes more and more resentful of the way she is treated by—*Beck*. Time and again he aims at her mind, her sick mind. He tries to analyze her ways of thinking, her distorted beliefs, and to demonstrate for the audience how a twisted mind can be fixed. He uses her to fill up a tape for sale. He is aiming at the core of her problem not with therapeutic, but with poisoned, arrows. He discards her intelligence, her thoughtfulness; he patronizes her (i.e., infantilizes her) and even comes down hard on her at a point when, discarding his maneuvers, she asserts herself and her intelligence. With the air of a knowledgeable expert he reflects back to her that "there are a few spaces that have to be filled in between intelligence and happiness. . . . " And the message is clear: she has not yet filled in those spaces; that is why she is in therapy. Presumably he knows what those spaces are or even possesses them himself.

I do not believe that in order for psychotherapy to flourish we have to produce myths, in this case the myth of happiness. But when one equates mental health with the appropriate beliefs, then happiness becomes a matter of actuality and one confuses the actual with the real. If one believes in happiness, this line of thought implies, then there is happiness. Anyway, this is not a happy hour either for Audrey or for Beck.

Beck is entirely oblivious to the interpersonal dimension of psychotherapy. To him Audrey is not a person but a disordered mind-person, an object. As the talk proceeds Audrey refers to the rape incident, but even then the expert is geared toward the "beliefs," entirely ignoring the *experience*. Furthermore, she refers to the rape incident in terms of being trapped and degraded. Beck, on the other hand, prefers helplessness: or in other words, he also degrades her on the spot by undoing her subjective experience. There is actually a short-circuit between these two people: while she is with *experience*, he is with *cognitions*. They are moving along parallel lines. This is vividly apparent when immediately after she refers to her experience of the rape, Beck interrupts the natural stream of her experience and says, "Audrey, you think we can take a look at some of these beliefs to see how well they fit and whether they might be more absolute or not absolute enough?" And he describes those beliefs and asks, "What is the evidence in favor of that?" The technique takes precedence over everything, even empathy—at least in this session.

What happens in the rest of the "conversation" is in fact a third-rate performance of a third-grade teacher–student interaction in an elementary school. Beck announces what the assumptions are and then asks the student to say, in order, what evidence she has in support of each assumption and what the proofs are that are contradictory to them. Audrey sighs at times, laughs ironically at other times, and furnishes plenty of evidence for and against each belief, like a good, compliant student. She knows very well the rules of the game, a game she is tired of but against which she cannot mobilize enough power to resist *directly*. She honestly says that she cannot assert herself in face of *authority*—her parents and later, parental figures who represent mainly intellectual authority—such as Beck. Nevertheless, she resists; she corrects his interpretations of her cognitions and thereby furnishes evidence that she can do a better job in that matter. And when at the end of the session for five long minutes Beck tries to extract from her a "piece of meat" in praise of himself, the therapy, and the cognitive method—Audrey tactfully and with her last drops of energy refuses.

What Beck has furnished us with in this session is a vivid demonstration of the abuse cycle that results when one adheres to a technique in which the therapist attributes to him or herself the faculty of *the knower*. Beck was not able to build a bridge to Audrey. He made her helpless to a greater degree.

The Second Session

This is an entirely different session. As we go along, it will become evident that things occurred in spite of the technique and not because of it, though Beck wants his audience to believe otherwise.

At the beginning, Beck ventures to analyze for the listener Audrey's behavior and personality as they were emerging out of the previous session, as well as to elaborate on the usage of cognitive therapy. It is a long and dry introduction. Beck dispenses intellectual awe toward his system of *"dysfunctional beliefs" correction* (i.e., cognitive therapy). We have a sophisticated system of "schemas," "matrixes," "structures" and "infrastructures," "evaluators" and "evaluations," "evidences pro and con," "straight empirical testing," etc.

And now pay attention to excerpts of an oration, and please take off your doctor hat and put on one of an ordinary citizen in a democratic society who to some extent is historically minded:

> In the interview we focus on the validity of their dysfunctional beliefs. These dysfunctional beliefs cause them problems . . . they are extreme, overgeneralized, and absolute. Once we have identified them, then we can evaluate them and proceed to make some tentative conclusions about testing and changing them. . . . In our first interview with them in order to determine the presence of their dysfunctional beliefs, we first look for the generality of beliefs across diverse situations, and evaluate them in terms of excessive or inappropriate reaction. In the second interview you will note that they are able to recall a few people who provide evidence contrary to their belief. . . . Part of this disconfirming evidence comes from their therapeutic relationship with Dr. (X). The accepting collaborative relationship provides the matrix for a corrective emotional experience. . . . They regard him as a friend. . . . There is obviously a change in their cognitive organization and their system of beliefs which positively affects their emotions and their behavior.

In the above excerpt I interchanged I with (we) and Audrey's name with (them), and changed the tense from past to present in order to give it a sense of immediacy. These are Beck's words. It is horrifying, and it is so because nobody would have agreed that such a systematized *thought* correction procedure would be used officially and with scientific backup with any free, ordinary citizen—unless, and that is the point, that citizen is alleged to be sick, mentally sick, with a twisted worldview that requires correction. We, and Audrey among us, do have absolutist beliefs. But the dread of those beliefs amounts to nothing in comparison to the dread afflicted by absolutistic thought systems, whether psychological or political-ideological. When such things are done in the name of psychotherapy, then it is conceivable that psychotherapy has fallen from grace and may be perceived as an enemy. In fact, psychotherapy, as such, is a formidable enemy. It has become a method/technique being used to *standardize thought,* in accordance, as I will claim, with simplistic conceptions and solutions to life's complexities, and a method used to *objectify persons.*

Who does the talking? Is it an excerpt from one of Orwell's writings? Is it a corrections officer addressing newly recruited officers who are presented with the mechanisms of thought-change the inmates must go through? Or is it an officer in a Cambodian corrections camp in which there is an absolute chasm between what one thinks, what one says one thinks, what one feels, what one says one feels, and how one behaves. Is this a place where one is supposed to go through a correction experience of *ideological conversion* (i.e., belief conversion) from which will ensue a positive change in emotions, according to the official ruling-class determination, which indicates total surrender, and also in behavior, which is necessary for order, which means for ruling (i.e., exerting power). And change, indeed, does occur. Millions adjust themselves to the ruling dogma, belief, ideology, whatever we may call these absolutist systems of ideas, to the extent of adopting a set of beliefs previously foreign to their being and believing it is their own set of beliefs. *This is the real and the actual pathology.*

When one comes to therapy, not in the sense mentioned above, one is sublimely declaring distress at this chasm between a "public self" and a "real self," using H. S. Sullivan's (1955) terminology. The majority of people are not bothered with this chasm and many have found a *conforming solution,* in contrast to a *creative, self-defined solution,* to this everlasting ontological problem.

At a time when the total population of the world approximates the amount of total ozone, a reminder of the difference between *things* and *persons* appears relevant. Things are determined by their nature, they do what their nature determines them to do. They are subject to their nature, and are not capable of surmounting that nature. They are not subject to what we persons call *choice. Persons,* on the other hand, within certain limits, can direct their tendencies and surmount their nature. An impulse-driven infant will mature and become a person as a result of a series of decisions and choices within a complex nature and nurture interaction. To the extent that a person is capable of making such serial choices and decisions, the individual ceases to be an infant, *a thing,* and becomes a *person with a personality.* A *thing* may have a *style* but never a *personality.* A piece of furniture may be styled after the baroque or the modern, etc., yet a chair is a chair forever.

Now, one may decide to style oneself after, say, Elvis Presley. The person is treating the self as a thing, as an object; yet a person is always capable of making other choices about what he or she will be and do. A *person* in contrast to *a thing* holds an immanent potentiality for becoming a unique personality. Totalitarian systems, whether political, ideological, philosophical, or psychological, aim at invalidating the *person with a personality* and replacing him or her with a *person with a style.* It is a sophisticated way of exerting control and power because the objectifying process is concealed and disguised. In our case the objectifying process is concealed under the guise of—a psychological science!

According to this "revolutionary" science (originally, the cognitive revolution in psychology had nothing to do with psychotherapy, and the later linkage of these new cognitive therapies with that cognitive revolution is a dubious one), there are specific dysfunctional styles ("patterns") of thinking characteristic of certain persons. In the good old days these were the melancholic, depressive persons, but nowadays, as the dynamic of any "revolutionary" creed deems, this one has been expanded and has become an imperium which comprises the vast domain of the Neurotics, the people with Personality Disorders, and even the uttermost Psychotics. This provides another illustration that no one is immune to "pathological thoughts"; it is not only the so-called "patients" who are prone to "overgeneralizations." And when a person is looked at as a cognitive object, then the person has been dehumanized and reduced to the level of a *thing*.

In attacking the physicalist's conceptions of objectivism, Kierkegaard (1938) noted:

> Usually the philosophers, like the majority of men, exist in quite different categories for everyday purposes from those in which they speculate, and console themselves with categories very different from those which they solemnly discuss. That is the origin of the mendacity and confusion which has invaded scientific thinking.
>
> In relation to their systems, most systematisers are like a man who builds an enormous castle and lives in a shack close by; they do not live in their own enormous systematic buildings. But spiritually that is a decisive objection.

Spiritually speaking, a man's thought must be the building in which he lives—otherwise, everything is topsy-turvy. (p. 156)

As we continue with the session with Audrey, it becomes evident that indeed some psychotherapists live in shacks close to their theoretical castles. As noted, this chasm is responsible, at least in part, for the unbridgeable gap among theory, research, and practice in psychotherapy. The state of the matter being as it is—it is indeed impossible to build a bridge between a shack and a castle—one wonders what is topsy-turvy and by how much. I believe that it is the enormous technical—theoretical castles that we have erected and with which we have wrapped ourselves that are responsible for psychotherapy's objectifying *itself*. Our technique is our *style*; on its glorification we dwell relentlessly. We are a *thing*. Once again the abuse cycle becomes evident: we, the therapists, treat ourselves as objects, and we are perceived as objects and are treated as such (a deus ex machina for providing a mental fix). They, the "patients," treat themselves also as objects and are treated as such as well. Audrey, and, as I believe, many "patients" in many other cases somehow manage—maybe because of their dread, and if they are listened to carefully and respectfully—to demonstrate for us that at least in the realm of interpersonal interaction there could be a bridge between the castle and the shack, between our *facade* and *style*, and our *personality*. Audrey was lucky. Beck could listen, eventually. Let us examine the process:

We understand that Audrey had been assigned some homework concerning "what we talked about last time." When I read the book *Cognitive Therapy of Depression* (Beck et al., 1979), I appreciated, and still do, the

fact that this system makes itself familiar to the client
by providing information through reading materials.
Thus it abolishes one of the two sources of power in
psychotherapy: *anonymity of the technique/system* (the
other being *anonymity of the therapist*). I thought that
the reader was being taught what are, for example, common modes of cognitive distortions, such as "all-or-
nothing thinking; overgeneralization; mental filtering;
jumping to conclusions; magnification, etc." (Burns,
1980), and then *the individual* is being asked to try to
depict if and when any of these are relevant to him or
her, and then bring it to the therapy session for discussion if one chooses to do so. But I have misjudged the
all-encompassing power of expertism and the alleged
knower. Look what had happened in fact:

B.:   *Audrey, thanks for coming back in again. I see you
       have some notes there, does this have to do with what
       we talked about last time?*

A.:   *Yes, it does.*

B.:   *Aha. So I think what I asked you last time was to test
       out some of your beliefs about yourself, such as: "I am
       powerless; I am an innocent victim; people can't be
       trusted; they just regard me as an object; I am
       trapped."* **You had a whole variety of thoughts like
       that, and beliefs.** *And what I wanted you to do is to
       see if there was evidence that supported that or there
       was evidence that contradicted that. And I think you
       are going to look for evidence that contradicted some
       of these beliefs.* [emphasis added]

A.:   [with a powerless and trembling voice]: *Ahh yes,
       that's true.*

B.:   *And . . . what do you have there, can you read it . . .*

A.:   *Ah yes, yes I can* [please pay attention to the scho-
        lastic manner of her presentation of the home-
        work]: *one item was working at evidence to support
        the notion that people do not regard me as a second-
        class citizen and fortunately there were several ex-
        amples. . . .*

First, it was Beck who asked Audrey to do some
homework. This is in accord with the principles of the
cognitive model of therapy. We do not know if Audrey
as a free person had the option of refusing either to do
the homework or to bring it up for discussion. But these
considerations are not as important as the question of
the *quality* of her homework: she was given a list, not
just a list, but a list of defects; not just a list, say, of
physical defects but *a list of ideological defects*. And she
was ordered by an authority to analyze them: Beck ex-
plicitly says he asked her to do this "homework," and
nobody would deny his position of authority which, in
the first place bestows on him the privileges he assumes.
The authority instructs the "degenerating" citizen to
go home and contemplate "a whole variety of thoughts
like that" (come up with what you like; ideally you have
removed your therapist hat and have minded yourself
historically), and to come back with new evidence to
the contrary. In this case you will qualify for acceptance
and approval. But if you do not realign, then you are
taking the risk of ostracism; you will be predetermined
as one who holds to the wrong beliefs—you are pathological.

What we witness here is in fact a system of thought
which is called, in our particular case, cognitive therapy,
and which provides a philosophical, scientific foundation to streamline individual thought and action into

fixed predetermined patterns. Again, what gives such systems the authority to exert their abusive power is the fact that first they label one as mentally inferior and then they offer remedial means for the condition. The source of power is the pathographizing process.

Speculating about what might have happened there and then between Audrey and Beck, I can easily detect some interpersonal, power-related dynamics. Remember that in the first interview Audrey was relatively belligerent and resisting as best she could in that particular authoritarian situation. She even demonstrated a high degree of knowledge and familiarity with the principles of cognitive therapy. Despite her inferior position and her sense of powerlessness in the face of intellectual authority figures, she resisted an expert's relentless efforts to use her as an object. In a way, she asserted herself, and assertiveness, you will recall, was her genuine presenting concern. If anybody was competent in that session, it was Audrey. But she took too great a risk. She, with her compliant rebelliousness, was on the verge of ruining a preplanned and highly invested project of demonstrating the effectiveness of cognitive therapy even with personality disorders. But foremost, she had shaken the authority of *the* authority. And the punishment was not long in coming: she was handed a list of her misbehaviors; sorry, misbeliefs. A patient should know her place.

At the beginning of this session we witness a woman whose pride has been crushed. She reads/voices submissively the lists of her sins (we sin in our thoughts also, don't we!), and provides the master with ample and touching evidence in favor of her new enlightened beliefs and in favor of the reeducational system. It seems she has given up. But she has not allowed the process of standardization to push her down. She manages to lift herself, and as a consequence also Beck, into something higher. And do not forget that she is the "patient"; she compels the expert to relate to her as a *person*, and not a *thing*.

While addressing her assignment she indicates that she is mistrustful of "various individuals who are appearing to be pleasant and nice to me [but] are actually doing that to deceive me and to ultimately hurt me or to use me in some way." This is the worst assumption she makes initially regarding people. At first, Beck tries, as the system deems, to challenge this core distorted belief and to demonstrate to her how she is making another generalization about situations. But Audrey is aiming otherwise. When he asks Audrey if she sees "that in all situations that you are going to," she answers, "Pretty much so," and adds that "if the individual is very aggressive I can say, okay, that is what that is," but she feels especially so with a person who appears very kind—the person-to-person encounter is inevitable. Beck has no other choice but to relate to the here-and-now and the interpersonal dimension of their interaction:

B.: *Did you feel that in regards to talking to me?*

A.: *Yes . . . yes . . .* [very much relieved]

B.: *What thoughts went through your mind . . . just . . . you spoke to me?*

A.: *Ah . . . well . . . I wish you were* [she sighs heavily]. *. . . Well . . . That is the case, hhh, . . . I . . . was . . . wondering of . . .* [very cautious, every word measured with dread], *my gracious . . . what . . . **what is the real person** . . .* [laughs out of bewilderment] *sitting right there and would your manner,*

> *would your behavior change suddenly leaving me vul-*
> *nerable. I would get accustomed . . . and . . . to you as*
> *you appeared to be and become relaxed and then I*
> *would just be totally not able to . . . to handle the situ-*
> *ations as it had changed . . .* [emphasis added]

Simply put, Audrey is saying, to an ear that is willing to hear, that she does not feel *safe* with Beck. She also challenges another source of power in psychotherapy—that of the *anonymity of the person therapist.* A person is concealed behind the *mask of a technique.* Accurately and with good judgment, Audrey senses that there is a gap. Again. A gap between what they say they are doing, in the name of her *well-being,* and what they are actually doing, in the name of the *technique or system.* She is confused and she wants to know what is "real." She accurately perceives the situation as unpredictable—accurately, I say, because it *is* the reality, it is not her so-called disorder. Throughout the sessions Beck has applied to her an *aggressive* system of mind surgery. To make a person a thing is the utmost embodiment of crude aggression, if not evil (that is what the victim of rape feels). As Audrey said (see above), explicit aggression is much easier to deal with than implicit concealed aggression. Some abuse in the name of love; others abuse in the name of curing.

What happens later between these two people demonstrates what I have mentioned about the alleged difference between us and our "patients"—that this difference in fact has been set up artificially. We, the prospective psychotherapists, were at a certain point of our life in a kind of psychological crisis, as is the person sitting in front of us now as a patient. Basically, the difference is in the way we chose to deal with this crisis in living. We chose to become therapists. We "cure" and are "cured" simultaneously. They chose to go into therapy. The choice had much to do with life conditions and opportunities. The difference is in no way a matter of quality: Audrey says she is scared of the same thing, the same attitude, she finds in Beck. She says she fears Beck will start yelling at her.

B.: *Would I have any reason for yelling at you?*
A.: [She makes desperate efforts to overcome her paralysis and to put into words her authentic feelings.] *Ahm . . . hh . . . if hh . . . hh if I my hh . . . the thought that pops into my mind . . . hh . . . if I happened to say something that sounded too intellectual, or whatever, you would want to yell at me and to put me in my place?*

Audrey and Beck have something in common: not only are they both intelligent persons, they also heavily rely on intellectual (cognitive) processes within interpersonal contexts. Audrey uses the same "technique" as Beck, to show those around her what a "knower" she is—how wise, competent, and effective she is. Of course, this is a form in which aggression is channeled, either by therapists or by others. That therapists are licensed to do that—via a host of symbols and emblems in praise of their intellectual assets—does not necessarily mean a metamorphosis of this aggression into benevolence. It only means that those therapists who need it have found a socially approved way for expressing their intellectual (and sometimes aggressive) needs. Audrey, though intelligent and with apparently a strong need for intellectual expression, is still in search of such an avenue. This is a difference in kind and not in quality.

Audrey was honest from the beginning. Very early she said that authoritative people do not let her put herself on the same level as they are, that they put her down, that they regard her as an object, etc. She observed how this had happened at her parental home, at her workplace, and in the city (when raped). Beck, as already mentioned, did not believe her beliefs, as was the case with our forefather Sigmund Freud, and as a result we witnessed an enactment in therapy of her reality. The abuse cycle has been completed.

Afterwards we bear witness to what are perhaps the only few minutes of genuine interaction in these sessions. Beck is obliged to abandon his technical power maneuvers and accept her challenge to be a person with her. He listens empathically and tries to understand. He *reflects* on her *feelings*—of frustration and powerlessness, and of not being able *to actualize* her *potential* and her "real value" ("You never really get a chance to show your own ability or creativity . . . achieve what your potential is . . . ") And he acknowledges—and this is important—that she has gone through traumatic, "painful" experiences. When he approves the reality of her subjective experience, the dam is broken. Fluently, affectionately, and fully experiencing, Audrey describes how as a child she spent hours just trying to get a loose tooth out lest she be punished severely by a mother who didn't like to be around her, who abused her physically and verbally; how she was not supposed to talk around the dinner table; how her mother was hostile to her by being *indifferent*. She recalls her mother's facial expression while bending to smell her hair which she, the mother, purposely had not washed for a couple of weeks: "Her look was awful . . . she would be repelled . . . repulsed . . . disgusted."

Here is another example of the aforementioned abusive pathographizing cycle: a child is being treated by her own stem family as *different*, just because of her darker complexion (remember the very beginning of the first session!). What happens when such a person comes to therapy? Yes, she is being treated again as *different*: sick, disordered in personality, twisted in mind (cognitions, beliefs, etc.). . . .

What, then, made possible—as Beck himself admits in his epilogue—this authentic and therapeutically meaningful testimony? *Empathy.* As said, some men build enormous castles but actually live in a shack—or should we say in another's shack—close by.

The rest of the interview adds nothing meaningful to our discussion. Beck, as a dutiful pupil of his own invention, returns to the routine duty of a correctional and a reeducating instructor who is checking and fixing dysfunctional beliefs and notions—except that now he introduces another item to the list of her sins: irrationality. Audrey also returns to her routine of complying, acting like a good and pleasing (nonrepulsive?) daughter in front of a powerful authority figure. Why "like"? Here it is: towards the end of the interview Beck ventures to display the benefits Audrey has accrued during her more than 6 years [!] of therapy at the clinic:

B.: *On the other hand you have made a lot of progress. You said when you first started at the clinic you didn't have a job at all and now you have had a job for how long?* [So who made the progress? She? Or the clinic?]

A.: *For 6 years.*

B.: *Ah . . . so you have had a job for quite a long time and you have been gradually getting up closer to the point where you can fulfill your real potential* [here it comes: the real point] *and in general are you feeling more content . . . aa . . . since you have been making this degree of progress?*

A.: [sighs . . .] *In a sense yes, in a sense no. I feel frustrated that I haven't been able to fulfill some of the promise that I once had years ago; that is frustrating to me, but on the other hand I certainly feel more content that I am now going from day to day.* [It seems that she has surpassed her teacher. Suddenly he asks for a "general" response. But she dislikes "all-or-nothing" responses, and her answer is a better example of what a balanced analytical and functional thought content should be.]

B.: *Yah.*

A.: *And some years ago I . . . that was my only goal.*

B.: *Yah. So, you don't have to live just one day at a time anymore.*

A.: *Right.*

B.: *Ah. That is very good . . . Well . . . it's good talking to you again Audrey. Thank you for coming again.*

A.: *Thank you.*

B.: *And we will see you again soon.*

A.: [unrecognized giggle]

As with the first interview, Audrey refuses a definitive answer as regards the efficacy of the cognitive model of therapy or if she is going to come back again.

In a review of trends in psychotherapy in the 1980s, Judd Marmor (1980) contends that the new cognitive therapies are simply repeating history. *"Plus sa change, plus c'est la même chose!"* (p. 413). The author claims that these new cognitive therapies are throwbacks to a pre-Freudian technique advanced by a Swiss psychiatrist, Paul Dubois, in the mid-19th century. Dubois called his method Rational Psychotherapy and based it on "curing the will through self-education" and on "modifying the erroneous ideas that the patient has allowed to creep into his mind" (Marmor, 1980). Judd Marmor remarks that even at that time, Dubois' rationalism was challenged by Joseph Dejerine, Professor of Psychiatry at the Salpétrière in Paris. And Dejerine put it this way:

> According to Dubois, psychotherapy ought to be "rational," that is, based solely on reason and argument. . . . If reason and argument were sufficient to change one's state of mind, the neuropaths would find in the writings of the moralists and philosophers . . . everything they would need to reconstruct their morale . . . and therefore they would have no need of a psychotherapist. Reasoning by itself is indifferent. . . . Psychotherapy depends wholly and exclusively upon the beneficial influence of one person on another. (As cited in Marmor, 1980, pp. 412–413)

In the 1940s, Henry A. Murray (1981), addressing a symposium of the American Psychological Association, observed that:

> Superficiality is the great sin of American Personology. It suits the tempo of the times; it suits our boyish optimism. And it suits the good heart of America, its Rotarian solidarity, its will to agree, since it is easier to agree about the surface than about the depths. Perhaps there are no depths. Who knows? There *are no* depths. Since truth is a congenial fiction, and *this* fiction is most congenial, *this is* truth. It is no mute thing that the inventor of behaviorism found his destiny in the advertising business. (p. 311)

Psychoanalysis provided a haven for Murray as a "contrast to all this shallowness." The reader will judge whether or not superficiality has been the great sin of cognitive therapy. But where can there be found a haven of protection from all this power abuse—for ourselves and for our clients?

CHAPTER FIVE

The Abuse Cycle

The significance of power, with which the social scientists, the historian, the economist, and others have been so familiar for decades, is only recently beginning to attract the attention of mental health practitioners, a very few of them; the majority, being in power, prefer to circumvent the challenge. The mental health system, represented by its organizations, collaborates with the current cultural systems, such as the educational, economical, industrial, and military systems, in propagating the view that the nature of the individual is untrustworthy, hence he or she should be directed, guided, rewarded, punished, and controlled by those who are wiser or higher in status. Mental helpers are *conformists* par excellance. But, as Rogers (1977) observes, "To be sure, we [mental health practitioners in general] give lip service to a democratic philosophy in which all power is vested in the people, but this philosophy is honored more in the breach than in the observance" (p. 9). In other words, it is a philosophy that means an illusion and, without getting into questions of cause and effect, this double reality might be partly responsible for our inability in "bridging the gap" (Talley, Strupp, & Butler, 1994) of the honorable obsolete triangle—psychotherapy theory-research-practice. What we do is not always, or is not often, what we claim we do, a gap which warrants, as Szasz (1968) recommends, careful study. This is a very well known fact in therapeutic circles, and to what extent this fact is ignored becomes clear when in 1991—23 years after Szasz, and Bergin and Strupp's (1972) warning—Holmes and Lindley (1991) still write that "what therapists do in sessions is often different from what they say or think they do" (p. 9).

Spence (1982) recognizes another gap, though from a different point of view. He distinguishes between narrative truth and historical truth, and reckons that in psychoanalytic literature, given the force of narrative tradition, clinical events are smoothed over "with the result that by the time it takes shape in process notes or published reports, it has acquired a narrative polish . . . we have no way of knowing whether they should be considered as true examples of the formulation or as overzealous attempts on the part of the reporting analyst to fit the findings to the theory" (pp. 26–27).

Another conspicuous gap usually mentioned off the record is the one between the image of the counselor you get from his or her writings or recordings and the image you get when you happen to meet the counselor in person. Yet another gap, revealed in unbiased biographies, is the one between the person-expert sitting on the couch and the one beyond therapy hours. Enlightened, one comes to acknowledge that the Latin poet Terence's utterance, "Nothing human is strange to me," is a matter of reciprocity comprising both parties, yet unknown to one side, the Other, who catches the expert's message, and is diagnosed to believe so, that he or she, unlike certain others including the expert-therapist, is the embodiment of all that is strange.

From the perspective of power and control these gaps should be maintained and sustained because they preserve the current reality and nourish the myths (throughout this book I follow the Aristotelian connotation of *myth* as fiction that disguises the truth about human life and the world) and values of those who benefit from them. In reassessing and reevaluating his work, Carl Rogers (1977) confessed that it took him years to recognize that the violent opposition to client-centered therapy sprang "primarily because it struck such an outrageous blow to the therapist's *power*. It was in its *politics* that it was most threatening" (p. 16). Rogers felt compelled to "confront openly a subject not often discussed: the issue of power and control in the so-called helping professions" (p. 6).

Power may be defined as the capacity to produce desired effects on others; it can be perceived in terms of mastery over self as well as over nature and other people (Heller, 1985; Wrong, 1980). A sense of power is essential to one's mental health; everyone needs it (Pinderhughes, 1989). Furthermore, we may even agree with Siu's (1979) suggestion that "power is the universal solvent of human relations" (p. 40). However, in agreement with this universal natural need, let me explore how the helping professions help in dispossessing a myriad of this same "universal solvent."

In *Moses and Monotheism*, Freud (1939/1950) declared his view regarding the question of power and control in the everyday world:

> The great majority of people have a strong need for authority which they can admire, to which they can submit, and which dominates and sometimes even ill treats them. We have learned from the psychology of the individual whence comes this need of the masses. It is the longing for the father that lives in each of us from his childhood days. (p. 12)

Assuming that power is a systemic phenomenon (Pinderhughes, 1989), and that "submission to power is the . . . earliest and most formative experience in human life" (Wrong, 1980, p. 3), a fact Freud definitely was aware of when he made the above statement, it is astonishing that he does not suggest any *radical* remedy to this need for dominance. He is satisfied with an explanation. A conservative, middle-class intellectual who adopted (i.e., adjusted to) the values of his contemporary ruling elite, Freud never was a social reformer. In this case Freud is a perfectly accurate phenomenologist who is not disturbed by a socioeconomic—some would also add racial—by-product which to this day entails dominance, subordination, and ill-treatment. Freud's view of groups is even more startling. Knowing *Mein Kempf* firsthand, out of my attraction for original primary sources, I can attest that Rogers' (1977) statement that it would almost seem that Hitler must have studied and adopted Freud's view is not an exaggeration. A brief quotation may suffice: "A group is an obedient herd, which could never live without a master. It has such a thirst for obedience that it submits instinctively to anyone who appoints himself as its master" (1921/1955, p. 33).

Was Freud right? Does the behavior of the masses in Nazi Germany and Fascist Italy serve as proof? Freud was wrong. Those events only prove what happens, and what might still happen in the future, when one who claims to be a master, by force of whatever justification—law, army, natural endowments, diplomas, etc.—dominates the scene of whatever nature. Domination and misuse of power in abusing others, often in the name of benefiting those others, whether materially or psychologically, are facilitated just because of that lack of equality, mutuality, and sense of communality. What Freud suggested was merely exchanging one domination for another, which he assumed to be more enlightened. This *mini*-changeover has had grave consequences, particularly for the helping professions, along three dimensions: *sociopolitical*, perception of the nature of *reality*, and the concept of *freedom*.

That therapy is politics is not a new idea; it is ignored, though, and in urgent need of periodic refreshment, as though there is an immanent resistance to deal with it on an ongoing basis as is incumbent on any political issue. Apparently, there are many good reasons to warrant such a massive mobilization of collective repression. Seymour Halleck (1971) thought that: "Any kind of psychiatric intervention . . . will have an impact upon the distribution of power within the various social systems in which the patient moves. In so far as politics is defined as the science of how power is sought, distributed, and exercised within social systems, all psychiatric intervention must be viewed as having political consequences" (p. 13). He agrees with the radical therapists when they insist that psychiatric neutrality is a myth, and proceeds to illustrate in his book why they are right. In full agreement with Halleck, I intend to proceed one step further in proposing that not only are we ignorant of our sociopolitical role—having become "only pragmatists [but not] dreamers with a vision of the future." Not only are we not geared to detect real socioenvironmental "oppressions" because of focusing on "internal systems," but psychotherapy actually has become an oppressive system in itself by duplicating and transferring (another example of the reciprocity of any abstraction) a power system and structure from the same environment from which a person seeks to be rescued. The objective should be how to make psychotherapy, I–thou interaction, *apolitical.* Then it would gain attractiveness, become an instrument for social change, and become trustworthy to many.

The heart of the matter is the question, not one of the "10 great unanswered questions of science," yet a great enough question and one that has answers: What causes people so much misery that they seek psychotherapy? It is a question of etiology.

Most psychotherapists, except behaviorists, contend that the primary source of misery is located in the person's internal system; that due to some unknown, unconscious, or unaware drives, feelings, thoughts, or fantasies, the patient alone creates his or her own misery. Psychopathology is the creation of the individual. This model of emotional misery, the traditional medico-analytic and its multitude of branches, confers some importance to other sources. But the sources are always secondary in nature, their purpose being to shed additional light on the present symptomatology. It assumes that somehow something is defective with this person; that something has gone wrong inside; that all is in the mind or, quoting a colleague: "What is outside is inside"!

Let us start with the reason of common sense. Practically, in contrast to the abstract, isn't there a worldly reality outside of our internal reality, which outstrips any fantasy, even the most fantastic internal ones, by distorting the most innocent and trivial realities in human existence? "It is a cliché," you may counter. But just open any newspaper any day of the year. It is reality, outside. There is no sense to science without common sense. Now we will turn to scientific data, first to history, what else, and then to empirical findings.

The source of this well-, and I might dare say also ill-ingrained notion of psychopathology is not, as one might instinctively assume, Freud, but his followers who canonized Freud and misunderstood his writings. Freud had no fewer than three theories of psychopathology. Giora (1991) expounds upon the development of Freudian thought concerning the three theories of the etiology of neurosis. He aims to dismiss the reality of the repressed unconscious which is not our concern here, but which I dealt with in the previous chapter from a different point of view—that of power. I will follow in some length the development of Freud's ideas because both bear implications important to our theses.

In his lecture on the etiology of hysteria before the Society of Psychiatry and Neurology in Vienna, Freud (1896) suggested that we "take our start from Joseph Breuer's momentous discovery: *the symptoms of hysteria (apart from the stigmata) are determined by certain experiences of the patient's which have operated in a traumatic fashion and which are being reproduced in his psychical life in the form of mnemonic symbols"* (as cited in Giora, 1991, p. 127). He also suggested that "The foundation for a neurosis . . . would always be laid in childhood by adults . . . " (p. 127). In a nutshell, this is Freud's first theory of neurosis.

What happened consequently is a lesson in the politics of power. As Giora continues to relate, Freud's lecture met with criticism, but not for scientific reasons. The chairman of the session, Kraft-Ebbing, author of the extremely popular *Psychopathia Sexualis* and numerous related publications, called it a scientific fairytale. He was reacting to the possibility that adults and relatives are capable of sexually attacking children and, consequently, turning them into hysterics. This is a fairytale, a fantasy characteristic of these patients, and physicians should not be gullible and relate to these fantasies as recollections of facts. Even Breuer joined the ranks of those who believed Freud was losing his grip on reality. "The medical community was offended by Freud. Breuer had now abandoned him. Lowenfeld, who had initially shown some interest, certainly more than other psychiatrists, seems to have attempted to persuade Freud to abandon the seduction hypothesis. As long as he held to the seduction theory, Freud was alone" (Masson, 1984, pp. 135–136). A year and a few months after this lecture, Freud informed Fliess that he had turned about; he agreed that his patients told him fantasies and not facts.

Had Freud not been oppressed, the whole theory and practice of psychiatry would have been different. Fear of being cast out and pointed to as one who is "suffering from moral insanity or paranoia scientifica," as he wrote to Fliess (Masson, 1984, p. 135), was intolerable even for a man of Freud's stature. Furthermore, the transition from traumas to fantasy as the core of psychic misery opened a deep chasm between the parties involved, on the fusion of which I toil in this work. The transition implied that the patient, his or her experiences, utterances, and facts of life as told by that person should not or could not be trusted. The abusive reality, on the other hand, and the fathers of the hysteric patients were if not trusted at least ignored. Is it still startling that the Wolf Man hid from Freud that he was anally abused by a member of his family? If we do not trust others why should they trust us, even if trust is a token we often, very often, throw toward our "patients" hoping to soften their resistance?

As we know, Freud then ventured to elaborate on the theory of the Oedipus complex. What is less known is that Freud, in fact, did not abandon the trauma theory. As Masson (1984) brilliantly shows, he declined from definite adherence to it because the whole building of psychoanalysis would collapse—in other words for political reasons. In one of his last writings Freud expressed his opinion that traumatic neuroses are a category of psychoneurotic psychopathology. In this connection Giora (1991) writes: "Psychoanalysts, but also many experts who would deny being Freudians, did their best to widen the gap beyond any chance of contamination between 'neuroses' and traumata. Traumata are responsible for some disorders of behavior, but not of 'neuroses,' for neuroses, as defined by Freud, are the results of an unconscious conflict between a fantasy and a resistance to this fantasy" (p. 141).

Fantasy, of whatever origin, to remind the reader, is a self-made product, usually believed to be not oriented to reality. Thus, it is believed that the patient is out of touch with reality—extremely so if the patient is psychotic, relatively moderately if the patient has some character/personality disorder, or relatively mildly if he or she is neurotic—and therapy should aim to close the gap between fantasy, neurosis or pathology, and reality. What reality? If we deny that pathology is rooted in trauma, from real and realistic events, if we deny that it is anchored in reality, we are actually denying the patient's reality. What is left is what is conceived to be the real reality, the one outside his or her projections (i.e., fantasies). Paradoxically, and against our very best intentions, the more we delve into the "internal," fantasies, projections, etc., the more we widen the gap between the patient's conceived fantasy and his or her reality and traumas. This means more distortions, more illusions, and, since we are talking about human beings, more suffering.

What does traumas mean? We know that as opposed to fantasy or any other internal makeup, it is not self-imposed. It is not a misery that the patient creates internally. Of course we do have fantasies, of being loved, cared for, treated empathically, honestly, and respectfully. At their root, these were needs. When they met coldness and indifference, the most prevalent normal pathologies on earth, ignored by the authors of the DSMs, they became wishes. When even the wishes were dashed on the steel wall, the cruelty of indifference, then fantasy was invented in direct relation to the degree of the coldness, and in absolute need of self-preservation. Listen to a piece of testimony:

> I knew what was in the air. A will-he, won't-he charge. But did I know what was in my mind? What I wanted? No. Or at least I didn't know then the important thing in my mind, which was that (at fourteen) I wanted to be held—by my daddy. The way six year olds are. Nevertheless, what I got in the end, just as I was finally, definitely, decidedly in my own bed and drifting off to sleep, was oral rape. But surely, at fourteen, I should have been capable of escaping, of preventing that. Of screaming, perhaps? Or, as one psychiatrist put it, of *biting*? Damn right. And I would have been, too, you bet, if I hadn't so carefully preserved a portion of my kid-self, wrapped nicely in tissue paper. That portion which held as tightly to a belief in the magical powers of fathers as to a stuffed animal. (Armstrong, 1978, p. 7)

But she did try to scream, to bite—later, when she decided to go for therapy. This is a moment of utmost importance, coerced by the circumstances, as I alleged earlier in this essay, being a moment of *protest.* She, and myriads like her, protest against real oppressors and oppressions, using Halleck's terminology. What happens when they start to talk about that? For many that means going to therapy. Paradoxically the very act which denotes health and the possibility for growth is also labeled as pathology and admission of some sort of sickness. They are retraumatized. The abuse cycle is complete.

Then, how many tell us, "I have come because I feel unfulfilled," or "I want to grow, I feel stuck," "I want to explore my potential." Instead we hear again and again, "I have problems," "They (parents, judge, school authorities, etc.) say I should come to therapy (=I have problems)," or a need for some other sort of psychopathological checkup. They are seen usually by a psychiatrist who diagnoses and labels them according to axis I, II, III, or IV. Usually the traumas are relegated to the lower axis, because we are interested mainly in our question, which is: What kind of "personality" structure has evolved due to traumatic and other environmental and genetic factors? Is it a personality disorder, or milder, or psychotic, and of what kind: narcissistic, obsessive-compulsive, bi-polar? Of course the use of "personality" in this context is misleading, because personality is a broad concept comprising also what is called psychopathology. Personality is more than psychopathology. This confusion has many adverse consequences: so many people who openly proclaim, "*I am* a manic-depressive," "*I am* an obsessive-compulsive," exchanging certain partial learned or genetic endowments with the *whole.* Many others exchange "*Who* I am" with "*What* I am" in search of an artificial entity to fill up their shaken identity. In faith with the spirit of this book, when I say many, I include among them the mental health practitioners who are looking for *what* they are and in particular those who have the same inclination as their so-called patients by being attuned to *what* the patient is and not *who* he or she is.

The same attitude of seeing the child as a "what," as a part person, as an instrument, was responsible for a crippled human being's abuse, in the above case sexually, of his own helpless child. Without the slightest intention to justify his deed, and those of others like him, I would like to pose the assumption that the socioeconomic reality today leads to us all being treated as objects. And it is also my conviction that deep inside many persons who resort to therapy, buried under layers of common yet strange terminology, dwells a cry, a protest against feelings of being treated as an object, and not as a whole. Some of these people we label as paranoid, in one way or another, and to others we are deaf.

If we would hear that protest, assuming that we are sensitive enough to the social dilemmas of our age, we would have to assume social responsibility, which means political responsibility. In other words, we would also become protesters, pro or con, but still protesters. However, in the long and pitiful process we have forgotten our own misery and that of our fellow human beings. Indeed, why shouldn't we, if we hold to the belief, and nourish it as I showed in chapter 1, that it is possible that one might choose this specialty for external reasons such as "I could control my working hours" (English, 1972, p. 80). If one ignores one's own misery, in sociopolitical and not only psychological terms, is one capable of being aware of others' misery? Some are lucky, for whatever reasons, while others, those I termed as separatists, join the current system, which rewards them abundantly, and they collaborate with it in converting the misery inflicted upon the person to misery inflicted from within the person. "When large numbers of people are 'afflicted' with unhappiness, they cannot all be defective. The causes of their suffering cannot be totally personal or anomalous; they must also be within the nature of the immediate social environment," says Halleck (1971, p. 28). The immediate social environment, to remind you, includes therapies that "display a lack of interest in social injustice. . . . Each shows an implicit acceptance of the political status quo. In brief, almost every therapy shows a certain lack of interest in the world" (Masson, 1988, p. 285). Therapies objectify, and are being objectified, by the prevailing socio-economic-political reality.

A Jungian analyst with whom I worked demonstrated how deep at times might be the lack of interest in the "real" world in contrast to focusing on the internal world. In a staff meeting, she admitted having difficulty in remembering the names of the young "patients": "When I meet them I apologize and I tell them, 'Don't be angry at me; I don't remember your names but I remember your dreams, each one of them, in detail.' " Of course she found some theory—psychology is full of them—to justify, in her opinion, "this kind of memory," but the separation between the worlds, the objectifying of her patients, and an autistic communication with the unconscious (the dreams) and not the people themselves, are pretty obvious. The tragedy is that the other party is made to believe that this is something benign, something in their interest, sort of: "She remembers my dream; I am important to her," which is far from being the truth. She could remember both a name and a dream, knowing that it is the dreamer who confers significance, if there is any, to the dream. According to our terms this person has been oppressed by having had an illusion forced on him or her, implicitly manipulating the person to believe it is the truth, by utilizing a power structure which relies on authority and the prestige of expertism. What makes this sort of power exertion even more oppressive is the fact that "the person who is oppressed but cannot identify its source is likely to react inappropriately" (Halleck, 1971, p. 23). I would add to Halleck's observation, that in our case, in psychotherapy, we are confronted with a much more adverse situation: not only does our "patient" not know the source of oppression, that person does not even know that he or she is being oppressed, believing the contrary. In my opinion, this is the most inauspicious issue in psychotherapy. I will argue that this plight causes an "inappropriate reaction" resulting in the prolongation beyond necessity of psychotherapy and leading to cost inefficiency.

Let me introduce another view on trauma, as an experience, an overwhelming one, but still an experience. The duration of the trauma itself might be short, as in cases of a devastating tornado or an accident, or long, as in cases of prolonged exposure to psychological abuse or any kind of prolonged agony. The list is vast and may include all the posttraumatic stresses (*without* the word disorder)—stress itself (such as wars; natural disasters; concentration camps; discrimination; unemployment; death of a beloved figure; organicity or any severe physical illness; being a child of mentally ill, alcoholic, or parents who are physically or psychologically abusive; immigration; moving [McCollum, 1990]; rape; and so forth) is stressing enough that we need not also make it a "Disorder."

Now, if you look carefully, and honestly, into this list, or any of your own composition, you may notice that none of us is an orphan. All of us go through crises. As we know, crisis is essential for growth. We all also pull out of crises. Even schizophrenia is a solution to a crisis, or to crises. Thus, the main issue is how we emerge out of a crisis, whether developmental or accidental. The morbid nature of the current sociopolitical reality is reflected in the simple fact that though our life revolves around love, death, power, and maturational processes, it is as if all the factors have conspired to deny their existence from our organized consciousness, leaving them in the hands of Universal Studios, commercial sources of knowledge, and intergenerational "communication." Traumas do not wait until we mature. They hit us at their own will. Most of us do not know how to face or how to cope with them. A small fraction of us seek professional help while the majority refrain. Of course, this state of affairs proves, again, that psychology failed to become a social–educational factor. Views delineated here point to some possible explanations.

Let me now close the cycle I opened at the beginning of this chapter, by rephrasing the question under inquiry: Why do so many people who need therapy (i.e., coping with questions of living), not go for it, and the relatively few who go for it, do so only when at an impasse, and even then half of them do not last more than four to six sessions (Goldstein, 1968)?

In the previous section I made a statement of problems, and intent, through explication of my personal academic and career biography, unfolding pertinent research questions. Concern, a universal sociological one in nature, was expressed over the fact that so many people, so many times, subdue their freedom of thought, their independence of thought and feeling. It was assumed that submission to power is the earliest most formative experience in human life; and abuse of power is the most prevalent source of human misery. Psychotherapy allies itself with the current sociopolitical sources of power, thus becoming a tool in implanting and conserving current class values and potentially becoming itself a source, another one, of power abuse. It was argued that psychotherapy, and the mental health profession in general, is especially prone to abuse of power. Some reasons for this propensity have been described and explained. It was argued that our profession at times is a contributor to and not a remedy for abuse—that actually, psychotherapy preserves a cycle of abuse, thus perpetuating a human predicament. This observation might explain why so many people who need therapy do not go for it, and those who go for it do so only when at an impasse. The cardinal question which was addressed was: Why is therapy perceived as an enemy?

Another question which overlaps the previous one pertains to an inquiry into the possibility that there exists a real humanistic approach to human suffering which eliminates concepts and practices that remove psychotherapy from being a human science, converting it to what at times becomes an implicit exercise in power. This approach is called psychobiography.

PART II

THE PSYCHOBIOGRAPHIC APPROACH TO PSYCHOTHERAPY

CHAPTER SIX

Psychotherapy and Psychobiography

I have to admit that initially I was sort of ashamed, if not fearful, of lumping together psychotherapy and psychobiography. Indeed, psychobiographies, like traditional biographies, are concerned with a very specific subject matter: the life course of the distinguished, whether eminent or infamous. Psychotherapy on the other hand is destined for all. Furthermore, psychobiography, biography, and psychohistory are concepts used interchangeably to denote both *writing* and writing from a very specific perspective, that of the past. When I introduced my first thoughts about psychobiography in front of a group of psychology students, one young woman complained, "Why are you interested in dead people?"—she was demonstrating an intuitive assumption that biography and related fields are concerned only with things past. The ancients did not make such a differentiation between life and history, nor did they have separate concepts for these. The Romans used *vita* or *vitae descriptio* and the Greeks used the combination of life, βίοσ, and writing, γράφειν (graphein). While biography, *vitae,* is of an old age, psychobiography and psychohistory are yet in their infancy, like psychology and psychotherapy. The reader might find that any historical sketch of either psychohistory or psychobiography (Africa, 1979; Hoffman, 1982, 1984; Lifton & Stroizer, 1984; McAdams & Ochberg, 1988; Runyan,

1988; Stroizer & Offer, 1985) attributes the beginning to 1910 with the publication of Freud's *Leonardo da Vinci and a Memory of His Childhood.*

Runyan (1988) argues that "the history of work in psychohistory and psychobiography can usefully be analyzed in terms of developments within seven or so partially autonomous traditions . . . within political science, academic psychology, psychoanalysis and psychiatry, the deMause group, history, literary psychobiography, and . . . a miscellaneous category including all other contributions" (p. 19). The psychoanalytic and psychiatric tradition applies psychoanalytic theory to history and biography, viewing psychobiography as psychoanalytic biography (Friedlander, 1978). Contributions in this field include, in addition to the work of Freud, Erik Erikson's *Young Man Luther: A Study in Psychoanalysis and History* (1958), which is perhaps still the best known in the field, along with his later study of Gandhi (Erikson, 1969); Robert Jay Lifton's (1973, 1986) studies of "shared themes" of groups of people sharing similar experiences, such as Vietnam veterans or Nazi doctors; and the work of a group of psychoanalysts connected with the Institute of Psychoanalysis in Chicago, including John Gedo (1972, 1983), and Moraitis and Pollock (1987), who were particularly active in psychohistory. The field of nonpsychoanalytic psychotherapy is not represented. This and other traditions in psychobiography, including "academic psychology," on which I will expand later because of its importance for psychobiographic psychotherapy, do not apply to psychobiography for therapeutic means, either as a concept or as a methodology.

A substantial contribution to psychobiography is the work of academic psychologists influenced by Henry

Murray, Gordon Allport (1961, 1968), Robert White (1975), and others at the Harvard Psychological Clinic in the 1930s and 1940s. These academic psychologists and their followers were interested in the study of personality development, and for years provided the foundation upon which I viewed a person's struggles within my *practice* in psychotherapy. With each person in therapy I encountered an irritating tension between personality theory embedded in the person, and psychotherapy–psychopathology theory. While in distress, I retreated again and again to the study of lives in search of some sense of understanding. That was when I realized the need for a synthesis of a biographical, psychological, sociological, and historical approach in understanding, versus analyzing, a person's lived life.

Recently a new approach to understanding human action has become popular in several domains of psychology. Narrative psychology might be added as the eighth to Runyan's seven traditions of psychobiography. Its roots are in hermeneutics (Ricoeur, 1970, 1976). Narrative theorists (Bruner, 1986; Freeman, 1993; Howard, 1989; Mair, 1988; McAdams, 1985; Polkinghorne, 1988; Sarbin, 1986; Spence, 1982) purport that "psychology is narrative" (Sarbin, 1986, p. 8). Mair (1988) holds the position that: "Stories are habitations. We live in and through stories. They conjure worlds. We do not know the world other than the story world. . . . We inhabit the great stories of our culture. We live through stories. We are *lived* by the stories of our race and place" (p. 127).

In accord with hermeneutics, narrative psychologists emphasize the link between identity or selfhood, and interpretation. The development of identity is viewed as an issue of life story construction; psychopathology as an instance of life stories gone awry; and psychotherapy as an exercise in story repair (see Howard, 1991). Retelling of life stories, or *"rewriting the self:* [is] the process by which one's past and indeed oneself is figured anew through interpretation" (Freeman, 1993, p. 3). Interpretation, by this tradition, is viewed on Batesonian lines—as a method of study of processes by which we make sense out of the world. Since objective reality is unknown, all acts of knowing require acts of interpretation.

We encounter a peculiar plight when we search for specific "exercises in story repair": The realm is dominated by psychoanalytically oriented psychotherapies (e.g., Schafer, 1992), that make use of interpretation in the psychoanalytic sense, or else the tradition is barren, or at best marginal, in terms of psychotherapeutic interventions. Nevertheless, the narrative tradition holds great possibilities for humanizing the discipline of psychology.

It seems that the narrative tradition might have implications for a cognitive revolution in psychology. Howard (1991) observes that "if one considers thinking as storytelling and if one sees cross-cultural differences as rooted in certain groups entertaining differing stories and roles within stories, then one might see some examples of psychotherapy as interesting cross-cultural experiences in story repair" (p. 194).

Michael White and David Epstein's (1990) *Narrative Means to Therapeutic Ends,* though a psychobiographic account only in spirit, embraces some promises for the field of life story psychotherapy. Relying heavily on Michel Foucault's analysis of power and knowledge, the authors propose measures to help "one uncover the details of the techniques of power that persons are being subjected to, subjecting themselves to, and subjecting others to" (p. 31). They use oral but mainly written traditions in "the generation of alternative stories that incorporate vital and previously neglected aspects of lived experience" (p. 31). Though I share many aspects of the authors' approach—such as the importance of written material, germane to a narrative tradition; the notion of "truth" borrowed from Foucault; and the acknowledgment that therapy might entertain a "strong possibility" for social control (p. 29)—there are some essential divergences from the psychobiographic approach I would like to delineate: (1) The authors make the assumption that people experience distress when the stories of their lives, as they or others have invented them, do not sufficiently represent their lived experience. Accordingly, narrative plays a central role in therapy. (2) In the psychobiographic approach to psychotherapy the person plays a central role in therapy, and (3) the psychobiographic approach takes place primarily within an interpersonal framework. Narrative therapy, by definition, is headed along a cognitive frame of reference. Narrative means are utilized for family therapy ends. The psychobiographic approach aims at the individual. (4) Narrative therapy admits the inevitable political nature of therapy, and yields suggestions for detection and unfolding of social traumatic oppressors. The psychobiographic approach is cued toward detection and unfolding of oppressive traumatic factors in the practice of psychotherapy, as well as in the social milieu. (5) Both approaches agree upon the centrality of language and communication in character formation. Narrative forms, as proposed by me, might become *a* means for personal redefinition in the psychobiographic approach to psychotherapy, or might be proposed but utilized only if dictated by the "text," the narrator, the source, the person. In narrative therapy, narrative forms are *the* means. In criticizing the metaphor of person as text, Gergen (1988) says: "The metaphor of person as text favors the conclusion that valid communication, correct interpretation, and genuine intimacy are all beyond human reach" (p. 49).

CHAPTER SEVEN

Technique vs. Approach

Psychobiographic Psychotherapy: A definition

Psychobiographic psychotherapy is an approach, which is anchored in life and in any and many systematic psychological knowledge bases, utilized within a framework of free, mutual, nonabusive, nonpathographizing, real interpersonal interaction, aimed at making sense of a person's unique life history.

We live in an era that praises technology and technical innovations as ends in themselves. Accordingly, the current scientific wisdom considers it true that the course of inquiry should be of "what specific therapeutic interventions produce specific changes in specific patients under specific conditions?" (Bergin & Strupp, 1972). This formulation by its nature stresses the centrality of specific therapies, and techniques used in alleviating a human being's suffering. Therapeutic outcome is a function of technical competence and patient characteristics. The relationship itself, in this formulation, is not so important, not even what is done within it. The therapist, the person therapist, if any room is left for the person, is expected to achieve a fair level of therapeutic (i.e., technical) skills. No wonder there is a proliferation of all sorts of "manuals"!

Psychotherapy consists of a tripartite matrix: the person and personality of the therapist, the person and

109

personality of the person seeking the therapist's services, and the interpersonal interaction between them.
Many times, the person therapist is abandoned and reduced, in the name of expertism, to a mere compilation
of systematic or nonsystematic, technical "tools." Since
the limits of therapeutic technique do not receive very
sustained attention, what then accounts for beneficial
change? In reviewing recent research on treatment out-
comes, Miller and Rollnick (1991) concluded that "in
sum, the way in which a therapist interacts with clients
appears to be nearly as important as—perhaps more
important than—the specific approach or school of
thought from which she or he operates" (p. 4). And,
with Cartwright (1981), Miller and Rollnick (1991) determine "that therapist *style,* a variable often ignored in
outcome research, is a major determinant of treatment
success" (p. 4; emphasis added).

It is my assertion that the specific approach or school
of thought might be intermingled with the therapist's
way of being in the world in a manner in which the two
are actually inseparable. In this case a therapist might
"choose" an approach because *its* way fits *his or her* way
of being in the world. This may result in the fact that
the therapist's interaction with a client is in itself a by-
product of the school/approach to which the therapist
adheres. We confront an internal contradiction and
confusion out of utilization of concepts that are interchangeable; the way the therapist interacts with clients
has become his or her technique, or vice versa. Somehow we espouse the very basics we disapprove of by letting the technique, or the specific school, conquer the
foreground masquerading as "style." Could "ways" or
styles be taught? Or are they a matter of personality
makeup? Either you have warmth or not, empathy or

not. If optimism on the part of the therapist ameliorates the chances of change, how can a basically nonoptimistic therapist precipitate change by adhering to a "strategy of optimism"? To what extent can these really be taught?

Psychobiographic psychotherapy is an approach, in the most expansive meaning of the term. As with the writer, or the biographer, who evolves, grows, and matures along with his or her subject matter, the psychobiographer invents "techniques" during and within interactions with a client. In this sense, it is a dynamic approach. Our therapist needs more than mastery of a specific method, biographic or otherwise. Because the therapist is involved in writing in vivo an actual biography, a lavish mixture of spontaneity, intuition, and creativity is needed. The ultimate technique is the therapist, and the personality of the therapist. The therapist is in a state of constant, genuine thirst for non–dogmatic knowledge in a quest to replace technology—means-ends expertise and the technical administration of society, with the practical—that is the cultivation of character and the deliberation of societal goals (Habermas, 1970, Woolfolk, Sass, & Messer, 1988). The replacement of the "practical" (in the Aristotelian sense) with the technical is still responsible for what Philippe Pinel (1745–1826) named *alienes,* the alienated, who populate the different wards of the world: the clinics and closed wards of the *alienistes*—those who treat alienated people (the term *psychiatrist* was coined at the beginning of the 19th century by the German psychiatrist Reil), and the open wards all around.

The psychobiographic approach to psychotherapy is a generative process. It involves transfer of knowledge

and experience. The therapist relies on internal resources, in a way that does not mean a technique woven
by participation in long and boring technical courses,
or a rented laboratory carted from client to client, but
a true knowledge acquired through intense intellectual
and experiential intimacy with learnedness, and the
Other's (i.e., the "patient's") and the therapist's own
psychobiography (i.e., his personal psychohistory).

Another "displacement" the psychobiographic psychotherapist is aware of is when the technical replaces
the relational, a case illuminating how, at times, technique and an insecure therapist's variables interact to
enhance his or her own sense of power. Here the relation does not dictate the nature of the "technique" to
be tentatively applied; instead a technique is first invented which dictates the rules of the relationship, and
eventually the nature of the relationship. What about
the fall of the Bastille and the cry that human conditions, mutually explored and agreed upon, should for-
mulate and dictate the rules? Instead, we read and hear
scholarly lessons like "Through transference we analyze
their personality structure"; "We need rules to elicit
transference resistance"; and when you push harder,
you hear, "Well, we need something to work with or
on, don't we?"—another example of *objectifying* of the
person in a technical society. Manipulation and sometimes also infantilization are embedded in the process
of objectifying. This suggests that resistance in the process of therapy might reflect actually a resistance on
the part of *the therapist* to check for overreliance on
technical maneuvers hiding behind the "expert" self.
However, the tendency to put the onus on the client is
ever present in psychoanalysis, as signaling a total

"trend of forces with *the patient* which oppose the process of ameliorative change" (Menninger 1958, p. 104; emphasis added), and, in cognitive therapy, as signaling a "confounding reluctance to yield anachronistic and debilitating self-statements" (Wolberg, 1988, p. 772).

CHAPTER EIGHT

Psychobiographic Psychotherapy

I believe that it is a misnomer to call "therapy" the process that transpires between two people in a unique context. The *Penguin Macquarie Dictionary* defines therapy as the "treatment of disease, disorder, defect, etc., as by some remedial or curative process." In my view nothing related to problems of living can be constructed as disease, and nothing done within our framework relates to "cure," but rather to how to cope with life. The term *psychotherapy* constructs a very specific reality, or realities, and implies in fact a hierarchy of realities, in which the predominant "reality," the "norm," is conceived as superior to and healthier than the reality of the person who comes for psychotherapy. The position of the "psychotherapist" in this hierarchy is apparently high and yields many benefits related to status. The history of humankind can be construed as a series of clashes between two or more distinct realities each aiming at ascendancy over the other. The claim that one reality is true and superior to the other is at the heart of racism, prejudice, and gender and ethnic–cultural discrimination. There are as many realities as there are people.

This is the most burdensome dilemma of our century (Rogers, 1980). For centuries individuals who claimed to perceive a different reality were condemned, persecuted, tortured, and killed. Today we condemn them by pathographizing them and sending them for a "remedial and curative process" of seeing the world, the "true reality" as we see it from a prism of a specific socioeconomic system, a religious or a scientific one, an oedipal or a cognitive one, a client-centered or a behavioral one. Rogers (1980) could anticipate the nature and meaning of such a "pragmatic" mentality. He bespeaks a historical memory crucial in the formation of my own psychological development and historical existence:

> Can we today afford the luxury of having *"a"* reality? Can we still preserve the belief that there is a "real world" upon whose definition we all agree? I am convinced that this is a luxury we *cannot* afford, a myth we dare not maintain. Only once in recent history has this been fully and successfully achieved. Millions of people were in complete agreement as to the nature of social and cultural reality—an agreement brought about by the mesmerizing influence of Hitler. This agreement about reality nearly marked the destruction of Western culture. (p. 104)

I will add that the above agreement on *a* definitive reality entailed a massive *systematic* massacre of 12 million women, men, and children. These are known facts, and their implications are too overwhelming not to be taken seriously. A science of psychology which, in a hermeneutic sense, is estranged from moral and practical issues of human existence; a science which does not debate the moral, historical, and political nature of its executive faculty (the practice of psychology in psychotherapy) this science is in a gradual estrangement with life, because those facts are not being taken seriously. At this point Rogers' (1980) query raises a second thought:

"Will psychologists continue to be peripheral to our society, or will we risk the danger of being a significant social factor?" (p. 257).

If the term *psychotherapy* is not adequate, then, what term should we use to represent the unique process we describe here? We are looking for a term which maximizes the mutual nature of the person-to-person encounter, on the one hand, and minimizes the pathographizing, hence diluting the power structure inherent in the nature of this same encounter. Viewed as such we could readily find a proper term from a host of terms in any dictionary. For example, we could term it *discourse, conversation, dialogue,* or *just talk.* We have a problem when we insist that the conversation should yield "curative" attributes. Anderson and Goolishian (1988) propose the notion of "therapeutic conversation." This term has some appeal, as White and Epstein (1990) observe, because " 'therapy' and 'conversation' are contradictory by definition" (p. 14); and though, the authors agree, "conversation" goes some way toward challenging the realities constructed by, and the mystification introduced by, the term *therapy,* nevertheless, they conceive the term as insufficient representation of *their* system of *Narrative Means to Therapeutic Ends.*

In our "system" we do offer a series of *conversations,* which if agreed upon, might pose the ongoing retrospective question of whether they contribute positively to the well-being of the parties involved. The term *conversation* best represents the unique process that we describe, and throughout this book it is synonymous with the familiar "scientific therapy." It is an egalitarian, nonjudgmental, hence humane term in the sense that every person, to a certain extent according to his or her personal experience and history, is familiar with it. We remember the simple while searching for and looking into the complex. At the initial phases of psychobiographic conversation we, the two parties, are concerned with elucidation of pathographizing and patronizing patterns intrinsic in the current notion of "psychotherapy." One of these patterns pertains to roles.

In order to make things tangible, I would like to ask you to think about a "patient" you have treated lately. Now, read this:

> The organism consists of an infinitely complex series of temporally related activities extending from birth to death. Because of the meaningful connection of sequences the life cycle of a single individual should be taken as a unit, the *long unit* of psychology. It is feasible to study the organism during one episode of its existence, but it should be recognized that this is but an arbitrarily selected part of the whole. The history of the organism *is* the organism. This proposition calls for biographical studies. (Murray et al., 1938, p. 39)

Being exposed to many "clinical" case presentations, I am familiar only with a few that pursue these lines of inquiry, recommended by Murray et al. (1938) in *Explorations in Personality*. Conversely, these presentations are laden with yet another theory, that of psychopathology. In the same vein is the extensive use of the *Thematic Apperception Test* (Murray, 1943) for diagnostic purposes, when the psychometrist may know little about the underlying theory of *personality*. Of course, in therapy we can also study the organism during or along one episode of its life; it is feasible, but on one condition; that it has been consciously chosen and agreed upon by both parties engaged in the therapeutic encounter. The following case demonstrates the point under scrutiny.

Max is a 44-year-old single male, who shares a family home with a partly physically disabled older single brother who actually nurtured Max after their mother suffered postpartum depressions after Max's birth and was hospitalized several times. Their mother and father are deceased. Max's hospitalization precipitated his request for therapy. He was unemployed for a couple of years, had apparently no friends and few interests. There was no unanimity about diagnosis—whether it had been schizophrenia, paranoid type, or chronic; or depression with psychotic features. He was motivated for therapy, and was cooperative and intelligent. Session after session, for 6 months, he would come to therapy drawing up the same complaint, though variously phrased: "Lately I have been depressed." Session after session we went through supportive or investigative behavior–cognitive therapy, looking into conditions of life to explain his dissatisfaction and into alternatives to alleviate his depressive mood. His complaints tenaciously recurred, and gradually yet consistently Max piled up anger over therapy not being therapeutic. Naturally, I was not left much behind him and felt the same frustration, and when in the next session he leased a new life to his aged complaint, I decided to face it directly. I asked Max how he felt about a therapy that did not help him. With honesty, as he had initially contracted, he said he was "very disappointed, and to tell you the truth, I feel a bit angry." With honesty, as I had initially contracted (on its nature I will expand later), I said that "I am also disappointed, and feel a lot angry." Max was staring at me with question and exclamation marks, but not for long: "You see," I said, "I have been seeing you for almost 7 months, week by week, yet I have no idea who you are, and I feel that you present to me only your pathology, only a specific part of who you are, and I *know* it is not what I intentionally elicit." An inward gaze replaced the stare, and Max sighed: "Yes, I don't know why I don't bring to therapy my *totality.*"

In this conversation, two shifts, or two therapeutic aims, if you prefer, have been achieved. First, the "patient" was addressed with a choice of taking himself either as a "short" unit, or as the "long" unit. There was an implicit agreement, one that is absent in behaviorally oriented therapies which presuppose that the study of the organism during one episode is therapeutic but not if arbitrarily chosen. In a psychobiographic approach, choice of an episode is not arbitrary as the choice is being addressed and an agreement is being achieved. The "patient" is the one who makes the decision pertaining to what "remedies" are personally "curative." This is definitely a proposition that is foreign to the medical model, but essential in a psychobiographic model of psychotherapy. Second, that moment of choice typifies a proposition for a biographical approach toward the person's existence, now and then. From that moment on we are dealing with a *biographer,* assisted in his or her inquiries by a *psychobiographer.*

What is this particular *biographer* doing? What is the nature of the biography?

Within the framework of traditional psychotherapy the nature of the patient's "doings" is embedded in and emanates from the definition of psychotherapy as "treatment of disease, disorder, defect." And various formulations yield the same common notion that "the goal of psychotherapy is to enable a person to satisfy his legitimate needs for affection, recognition, sense of mastery and the like through helping him to correct the maladaptive attitudes, emotions, and behavior which impede the attainment of such satisfactions" (Frank, 1979, p. 5). Should we still wonder that "patients" cut through the "short" *unit* of psychology! A psychobiographic approach concedes the tasks of enabling and correcting the maladaptive to the person coming for help. The person is not engaged in a process of correcting maladaptive attitudes, but rather is conceived as "a playwright constructing a dramatic narrative to make sense of life" (Tomkins quoted in McAdams, 1988, p. 8). A person is not conceived of as a patient but as a *biographer*. It is a person-centered system, a full organism or personality, not a partial patient, self, or ego. With this change, a real and meaningful transformation takes effect in which there is no authoritarian "one-up," the expert, pounding the truth into a defiant "one down," the patient. The process under scrutiny is what a life history may say about both the person and the society in which that person lives.

Now I turn to the role of the psychobiographer, the traditional psychotherapist. But before that, let me finish our story about Max. In the following sessions Max's depression, naturally, still declared a firm presence, but the nature of his depressive complaints had been changed by being viewed and experienced as a particle within a whole, hence releasing much room for other issues in his life story. At times he asked for a drink of water, invited me to join him in relaxed smoking while talking about himself, and could even laugh humorously while telling me about his delusions during his acute episode. Maybe he had his first friend in his post-hospitalization era (see Rogers, 1980; Schofield, 1964).

CHAPTER NINE

Psychobiography as Synthesis

I defined psychobiographic psychotherapy as an approach which is anchored in life and in any and many systematic psychological knowledge bases.

This formulation calls for a new understanding which reshapes the role of the therapist, and it relates to the concept of "integration." A human being in the role of scientist or artist, at times, has to disregard what is known in order to allow, or to create, a new integration. Integration can easily turn to rigidity. Paranoia can serve as an example of the utmost integration, yet it is rigid. Or, as an another example, the psychotic individual is more of an integrated human being than the conformist whom Laing (1982) brands as mad. What is important, then, is the degree of elasticity, and not the degree of integration. Elasticity precludes reductionism—that life is not reducible to any one school of thought or belief system. Elasticity denies dogma. The implications for a theory and practice of psychotherapy are apparent.

Formerly, I made the assumption that psychotherapists choose their profession because they themselves have been inflicted with some kind of psychological wound. To this initial motivation, which is wrapped up in many, diverse, and creative intellectual and nonintellectual forms, we may add a necessary condition: a real and genuine interest in people, and not just an interest in the mere study, or the mere psychology, of people. One becomes a psychotherapist if while on the road to self-discovery others are also discovered, to whom the individual pays the same amount, but not necessarily the same *form,* of attention. The healthy psychotherapist realizes that, for example, psychoanalysis may have augmented internal self-awareness, but also that this same explanatory system might be detrimental to the understanding of the other's life history. This realization impels familiarity with many streams of thought, any of which might help shed light on a person's life, at a given personal historical moment, or on the whole. To quote Mark Twain, "when your tool is a hammer, then every problem is a nail."

Psychobiography as an approach for self-inquiry, and dialogue aims at finding the nature and underlying meanings of important personal and human experiences, in our case the biographer's experience as it is unfolded through his or her personal history. As such it derives knowledge from many schools, each viewing human experience from a different frame of reference, such as personality theory, client-centered therapy theory, psychodynamic theory, existentialism, learning and cognitive theory, psychopathology theory, literature, history, philosophy, and religion.

Should a psychobiographer be an "expert," say, in religion? Paul Abramson (1992), in order to understand the experience of a Russian Jewish immigrant, had to study the Jewish religion and rituals; otherwise, he felt, important information about the immigrant's formative influences might have been lost. Openness to a person's formative context(s) enriches the person psychobiographer, and supplies that person with important cues in coauthoring healing life stories (Schafer, 1981; Spence,

1982). The psychobiographic approach to psychotherapy recognizes the place and the unity of intellect-emotion-spirit. It asks: what kinds of psychological theory can be used, and in what ways, for understanding the course of an individual's life? In contesting the psychoanalytic view of sexual desires as the root of neurotic behavior, Giora (1991) says:

> Life as reflected in novels [and in every person's novel], as a rule, revolves around love, real and imagined. Newspapers and history books speak of vanity and thirst for power, of wealth and poverty, of famine and violence. Life is not just this or that, but all of these. Any attempt to reduce the bewildering multitude of life phenomena to one grain of essence cannot but do injustice to the greatness of the puzzle, or shall I say: mystery that we are living and observing. . . . Wounds of every kind, and not only of Oedipal origin, may hamper one from accepting and performing one's role in this drama. (p. 150)

Psychotherapy might be conceived, and practically used, as I will demonstrate later, as an opportunity to make up for what the educational system has failed in for centuries. I like to see psychotherapy as analogous to a Chinese character which stands both for "crisis" and "opportunity"—that the difficult crisis of a person would represent an equally important opportunity to become a student of human nature and learn about feelings, psychological development, and the nature and essence of life, all marginally dealt with in an estranged and irrelevant political educational system. I am reminded of John Dewey (1938) for whom education, experience, and life were inextricably intertwined. In its general sense, to study education is to study experience, which in turn means to study life. Sarason's (1988) autobiography synthesizes Dewey's view when he states that his life as a psychologist and his life at large—for example, customs, habits, rituals, routines, metaphors, legends, and everyday actions—are intertwined. Sarason does not fail to make a distinction between his vocation as a psychologist and the rest of his life, yet he recognizes that it is impossible to separate them in practice, because he is a human being as a psychologist and he is a psychologist as a human being. He, we, are an experiential whole. A theory of psychotherapy, as well as the practice of psychotherapy, should be anchored first and foremost in the everyday practice of life.

In sum, psychobiographic psychotherapy adheres to creative synthesis of current pertinent psychological knowledge.

CHAPTER TEN

The Question of Liberty in Psychotherapy

I mentioned a framework of free, mutual, nonabusive, nonpathographizing real interpersonal interactions. Let me now examine these propositions, while acknowledging the debt I owe to two of my teachers, Yehuda Fried (1978, 1984) and Zvi Giora (1988, 1991).

What is psychopathology? Literally, it is the science of mental disorders: psyche—mental; pathology—study of disorders. We have just translated words, exchanging a word for words. In order to have a better understanding of the concept, beyond its descriptive definition, we need to clarify its origin, and the way it came into existence. We need some historical background. We will learn, then, that we need to ask another question, because psychiatry preceded its basic science—psychopathology—by almost a century. So we need to inquire about the historical background of psychiatry.

As a profession, psychiatry came into being during the French Revolution, and its history is related to the history of madness. Philippe Pinel, a Parisian physician during the French Revolution, had his finger on the pulse of our arrant attitude toward psychiatric patients. He viewed psychiatric patients not only as people afflicted with a cerebral illness, but also as people who are alienated from their human nature, and as a contemporary, he treated them accordingly: an alienated

127

person is a person who is alienated from freedom. A free person, according to Pinel, is capable of assuming responsibility over his or her fate and life, while the mentally ill person is not capable of making such decisions. Treatment, said Pinel, should aim not only at curing cerebral disease, but at helping people become human beings (i.e., free people). He proposed a new setting for treatment of these "mad" people, and thus the first psychiatric hospital came into being, and with it, modern psychiatry (Foucault, 1961; Fried, 1978).

In the age of Prozac and a pill for every dis-ease, such a historical note might seem anachronistic, yet it illuminates how far a science has headed from its origins, becoming alienated to its nature. We will leave aside the question whether the transition from liberty and human nature to medicine was out of necessity, or incidental. What is important to our discussion is the fact that psychopathology and philosophy—human nature, and the question of liberty—are intertwined. Indeed, the philosopher Immanuel Kant (1724–1804), who at one time was much interested in psychiatric matters, believed that because mentally ill persons are not responsible for their own doings, and because responsibility is a matter of freedom, then philosophers, and not physicians, should delve into the problems, those related to freedom, of the mentally sick. Psychology, as an independent discipline, did not yet exist, but as a philosophical psychology (Boring, 1957), these problems of human existence were within its domain. They were, and they still are, even though the ideas of the French Revolution, and its American counterpart, are echoing dimly due either to the shortness of human memory or the development of a much more complicated society ruled by technology.

How does psychology, a science, intersect with freedom? Piaget (1965) said that science does not concern itself with two issues which are in the domain of philosophy, namely, God and freedom. Yet, these two elements intersect in the concept of *autonomy* (see Fried, 1984, p. 67), which is within the domain of science, and thus within the domain of psychology. We are familiar with this concept from the writings of Immanuel Kant. For Kant, the idea of freedom is inseparably connected with the concept of autonomy, and this again with the universal principle of morality. He talked about two kinds of behavior characterizing human beings. One he called heteronomous, a behavior originating from outside, from an external power, and the other autonomous, emanating from within, internal, and independent. When one behaves morally, but the morality has been procured from the church, for example, Kant would claim that that individual owns heteronomous morality. But when it has been procured independently by the person from his or her own set of values, Kant would claim that the person owns autonomous morality, which for Kant is the real morality, which has been made possible because of a person's freedom. Emanating from outside, the heteronomous morality is not morality, but dictation.

Piaget, as a scientist, devoted himself to inquiry into the concept of autonomy. He was much concerned with questions of moral development, and what he discovered was somewhat different (yet meaningful), from the Kantian dichotomy of the individual. He discovered that autonomous morality germinates in an individual only when the person is among other individuals who are together within a particular interrelated context—that of mutual obligation of the group. Thus, (1) autonomy, as Piaget implies, is developmental, and (2) "A developing autonomy from its lower median is 'we,' and from its upper median—'I' " (Fried, 1984, p. 68).

While Pinel was responsible for humanizing the sick, the mentally ill, another person, half a century later, became responsible for humanizing mental disease, mental sickness: Sigmund Freud. I refer to his conception of *continuum*, which is one of the most significant, if not the greatest, of Freud's contributions to the understanding of psychopathology in particular and to humankind in general. He claimed that a sharp dividing line between "normal" and "abnormal" behavior does not exist. There exists only a continuum from normal to neurotic, and from neurotic to psychotic.

But, is it a unidirectional and linear continuum, as Freud implied? In clinical reality, we know of people who have made transitions from normal to psychotic, passing over the neurotic state. Many psychotics return to normality without an intermediate neurotic stage. It is a clinical misconception that psychosis is a chronic and incurable disease—there are many instances in which one who was in a state of active psychosis ceased to be psychotic, and resumed a normal life without going through a neurotic stage. I know personally of several cases, and they are not "in remission," which is a concept that implies chronicity.

Fried (1978) suggests a two-way continuum much like a triangle. On one apex, normality; on the second, neuroticism; on the third, psychosis. Transitions are possible in all directions. Freud's contribution, and Fried's emendation, taken together with Pinel's spirit, support further humanizing "mental illness," and thereby the "mentally ill" and psychotherapy. What these three in effect say is that each of us at one and the same time is healthy and ill, normal, neurotic, and psychotic by imperceptible or differing degrees. Anyone who has, for example, been "in love" can attest to the fluidity of the above continuum, and to the problem of demarcation. There are other "problems in living" from which none of us is immune, and which demand a shift in our position along the continuum. A hurtful divorce, a serious financial loss, loss of a loved one, a sudden severe illness or a prolonged one, bombardment of several problems at once. What about those moments, sometimes long moments, in which we are not "psychotic" but behave in the "spirit" of psychosis, sort of saying "Oh my God" voicelessly: how did I lose my *mind*, my judgment, control? Madness is embedded in human nature. And if sparks of madness dwell in each of us, why do we scorn the "mad"?

Two hundred years after Pinel, this same question in a different guise still prevails with the same or greater magnitude. We need to be reminded that psychiatry was born on the foundations of the French Revolution and the notion that freedom is embedded in human nature. It was not born in any drug laboratory, genetic engineering experimentation, in any electroconvulsive machinery, nor in any laboratory of psychological interpretation. Affinity with predecessors does not always guarantee great strides as it did in the case of humanizing psychotherapy—the ways we handle people (i.e., ourselves). Let us examine, for example, what the current wisdom has to say about autonomy.

Psychotherapy derives its meaning from a definition of mental health which is a derivative of the definition of psychology. Psychology inquires into behavior, that is, life phenomena which entail cognition. Behavior, as opposed to reflex, implies will and choice. When we can will, and make a decision based on possible choices, we feel that we are in control of our fate, we are autonomous. If our sense of autonomy is endangered, or if we are deprived of it, we feel helpless, with concurrent depression and anxiety. The objective of psychotherapy is to restore the equilibrium that existed between the lower and upper part of the aforementioned autonomy median: a functioning and autonomous person. Now we can define mental health as an existing sense of control and autonomy, while sensing a collapse of it, or while anticipating such a collapse denotes mental distress or psychopathology (Giora, 1988). Freud himself (1926/1959) described such an experience of helplessness as trauma.

Giora (1988) cites many authors to prove that though phenomenologically different, all the neurotic disorders share a common basis: violation of the sense of control and autonomy. From this point of view, the psychodynamic notion of neurosis being a conflict between an instinct threatening discharge and defense against its discharge is a possibility, but not a necessity. For Giora, the genesis of behavioral disorders is in cognitive styles, and not drives. I might add the possibility of relational difficulties and the corresponding attachment styles.

A psychobiographic approach to psychotherapy intersects with the question of liberty in many ways. I prefer the term *liberty* because it is a comprehensive concept; it contains the notion of freedom being embedded in human nature, and as a human being's basic and natural right; and it contains the notion of autonomy as a motivating force, acquired through active search. It is an egalitarian, nonsectarian notion. It implies a relational setting based on mutuality. Bringing the concept of autonomy back to the foreground contributes to humanizing psychotherapy.

Talking about freedom instantly raises the danger of coercion. As said before, autonomy is developmental, and it occurs within the context of human relatedness. The danger is when at a certain point one comes to believe that one knows how people should feel, think, and behave; how they should be redeemed, as one understands the concept of redemption for them. That is imposing on others a value system which by now has attained the validity of being a universal law.

Dialogue, in the Buberian sense, stands in opposition to coercion and imposition, and ensures that one will not become a Fascist, or a political or religious or psychological totalitarian. Dialogue, to remind ourselves, is between people, persons; not their shadows, atoms, or transferential imagos. Dialogue is antagonist to personality adoration, idolization, and cultism. A person enters therapy not because "he needs us to tell him what to do, otherwise he would not have come to therapy," but because the person is faced with existential problems, or because of a state of mind of "demoralization," of "feelings of impotence, isolation, and despair. The person's self-esteem is damaged" (Frank, 1974, p. 271). Faced with helplessness and loss of a sense of autonomy, the person is in need of a psychotherapy that aims to heighten the person's "sense of mastery over the inner and outer forces . . . " (p. 272).

In this "state of mind" the last thing a person needs "to know" is that there is yet another inner force of which he or she was not aware—that of unconscious contents—which is in command of the person's feelings and behavior; which is wise (not him or her); which is the real knower (not him or her). Despite being amidst a turmoil, the person is capable of launching a healthy protest and can resist the course of this action. Brehm (1966), and Brehm and Brehm (1981) demonstrate that resistance is a "psychological reactance" to be expected when a person perceives that his or her personal freedom is being limited or threatened. This reaction is particularly strong when at stake is a topic about which the person is ambivalent (Miller, 1983), such as seeking psychological help. The person's feeling that somehow he or she is "getting through" to the therapist is what makes a therapist a powerful influencer. The person's resistance to being "cut through" is what makes a therapist a powerful abuser.

The nature of this "getting through" is the subject of the following chapter.

CHAPTER ELEVEN

Real Interpersonal Interaction

> Neither love nor insight alone cures. . . . What is therapeutic, when it is achieved, is "the moment of real meeting" of two persons as a new transforming experience for one of them, which is, as Laing said (1965), "Not what happened before [i.e., transference] but what has never happened before [i.e., a new experience of relationship]."
>
> (Guntrip, 1968, p. 353)

Here Guntrip acknowledges that there is something beyond even love, beyond even the once or still held powerful insight, and beyond the great discovery of transference phenomena by Freud. Guntrip seems quite radical in his point of view. He auspiciously quotes R. D. Laing (1965) who a few years earlier blamed object relations theory, Guntrip's included, for dealing with "objects," not "persons." And he is talking about "real meeting." But, an analysis of Guntrip's book reveals some curious subtleties. Guntrip is advocating *moments* of "real meeting." What happens after and certainly before those precious rare moments is "based on no real relationship between them [the physician and the patient]" (Freud, 1910/1957, p. 51); that is, it is based on transference. Obviously Guntrip translates Laing's

"Not what happened before" as transference relationships out of his own personal psychoanalytically oriented world view. Laing admits that he "was influenced
by Freud more than by any other psychiatrist or anyone
else in psychiatry" (Cohen, 1977, p. 203), but he persistently refrains from using psychoanalytic terminology,
not because of taste but because of substance.

Three years later Guntrip is decisive. It seems he
has heard Laing's criticism. He defines "the science of
psychodynamics" as a science that handles its own
unique phenomena, "those of our subjective experiences of ourselves and of one another as 'persons in
relationship' " (1971, p. 178)—not *objects* in relationship, but *persons.* Then why the quotation marks, you
may wonder! Because as opposed to Laing, here the
change of vocabulary is not a matter of substance. The
scope of transference is broader than the field of psychotherapy. There are no real interpersonal relationships on this planet, and as Freud put it eloquently,
transference "is a universal phenomenon." Nevertheless, Guntrip should be hailed for a welcome emendation to the psychoanalytic–psychodynamic theory of
psychotherapy. A psychobiographic approach to psychotherapy, on the other hand, assumes that it is the ongoing, as opposed to moments, of *real,* as opposed to
fantasized (and/or technical), *mutual* interpersonal relationships that make therapy therapeutic.

Of course, nobody would deny the existence of
learned patterns of relating (i.e., transference); personality consists mainly of these patterns formatted
throughout development through meeting people. In
the therapeutic situation the problem is how we determine which is which, and more important, *who* decides
which is which. In psychodynamic therapy, in particular,

and in any other psychotherapeutic discipline which is established upon expertism, in general, the therapist, the expert, is assigned the role of the ultimate and definitive arbitrator. The therapist is the one who decides whether a particular pattern of his or her relationship with the other person stems from the real here and now relationship, or replaces an earlier person with the person of the therapist; whether it is an accurate perception of real occurrences in the therapy session or in the person therapist in relationship, or it is a cognitive–perceptual distortion on the side of the "patient."

In the psychobiographic approach to psychotherapy this is a mutual task stemming from dialogue between two people. Any perception pertaining to the quality of the relationship, any interpretation of its ingredients, is based upon agreement. The two involved parties provide the criteria for differentiating between actual, "real," and learned, "transference," affections. After 2 months of therapy, Mark, approaching his thirties, who as a child had been sexually abused by a male relative, and who was overwhelmed by fears of male sexual assaults, started to fear my having the same intentions toward him. After a while, his fears being persistent, I addressed him by saying: "I am thinking about your fears of being sexually abused by me. These are your real feelings. I understand them, though I do not agree with them. I wish there was an objective way to make our relationship safe for you, but there is not, except my word, or can you think of anything else?" Fortunately, after only 2 months, he felt safe enough not to end therapy, and said that perhaps we should leave it for time to prove my intentions, and that in any case, pointing to his fist, "I can defend myself."

We had reached an agreement, first, that relationship is a *process* and, second, that he is not, at least in
the current relationship, helpless. A couple of months
later when the pendulum had been reversed, I could
use, in the name of mutuality, the same argument, "I
can defend myself," and proceed to other meaningful
issues pertaining to his gender identity. By the way,
through all these months he was fully aware, and this
time I agreed with him also, that he might be inter-
changing his feelings toward me with those toward his
abusing relative and other male figures. He himself held
to that interpretation. Nevertheless, this cognitive
awareness, this consciousness, did not derogate his intense feelings of fear toward me, until we set in motion
the above-mentioned criteria.

This brings me to discuss another related issue, and
I use again Guntrip's (1968) formulation as representative of a trend of thought in, but not only in, psychodynamic psychotherapy. "At the deepest level,
psychotherapy is replacement therapy, providing for the
patient what the mother failed to provide at the beginning of life" (p. 191). This is a powerful passage reflecting on the magnitude of the missions that therapy
systems have bestowed on themselves, and on the life
philosophy cornerstones of these systems. A feminist
point of view would argue, with justice, why blame mothers, who themselves are being failed by a male-domi-
nated social order? The above passage, as it is or in its
modified versions, illustrates what I described before as
reversing the spotlights from the main avenue of an
indifferent social order which perpetuates degrees of
abuse and victimization. Conditions of life fail us, including the "mothers." Contrary to the above passage,
let us bear in mind one from Virginia Woolf's (1938)

Three Guineas: "The public and private worlds are insep-arably connected . . . the tyrannies and servilities of one are the tyrannies and servilities of the other" (p. 142).

The therapeutic mission as exhorted by such philos-ophies of therapy entails, by definition, a megalomaniac stand, if not spirit, leading to an attitude of patronage, authoritarianism, and infantilization.

What, then, does therapy, a psychobiographic one, provide?

First, and foremost, it provides a relationship. "I be-come," says Martin Buber (1958), "through my relation to the *thou;* as I become *I,* I say *Thou.* . . . All real living is meeting" (p. 11). Carl Rogers (1957), believed that "significant positive personality change does not occur except in a relationship" (p. 96). In Rogers' view, this is one of six necessary and sufficient conditions of thera-peutic personality change. Alfred Adler and Harry Stack Sullivan claimed that psychopathology is primarily a dis-order in the realm of interpersonal relationships, which deserves to be studied on its own. All these approaches hold several common constituents at the base of which is the concept of *meeting.* A meeting becomes "real" when there is a dialogue, conversation, and when "there is no substitute for experience, none at all . . . words, labels, concepts, symbols, theories, formulas, sci-ences—all are useful only because people already knew them experientially" (Maslow, 1966, pp. 45–46). Ther-apy, then, must be an experience—in interpersonal re-lationship and conversation; it should be a real meeting. And, only the person can validly provide portrayals of his or her experiences in perceptions, feelings, thoughts and senses: the person is the knower.

Throughout this book I have made an effort to study components relating to power which hold promise for transforming the therapeutic relationship into a humane and real experience. I have tried to treat "real" along different dimensions: living practice and action (i.e., life) and the living practitioner (i.e., the person therapist, the psychobiographer). To the latter I want to refer with further comments.

I remember vividly my beginnings as a clinician when I held a firm belief in some rational order in life, and in living people as ultimately rational beings. Today it is a desideratum, then it was an axiom. Accordingly, I believed I would be able to instigate growth and health in people I met in clinics if I showed them their self-defeating patterns of rivalry, or whatever else, which originated in their parental homes. But gradually I came to understand that I was preaching to the choir: they already were enlightened with that knowledge! It was their tragedy, yet also their beauty, that they were sensitized to subtleties of human interactions. "Do you think I don't know that!" Iris rebuked me angrily, "He [her father] always looked up to me. He would refuse sometimes but, I knew, it was a matter of gesture, that ultimately I'd get what I wanted. She [her mother] was somehow pushed aside. But I have nothing to do with that. Do I? You see, at least I could rely on him; he could *give* me . . . things being as they were, I know my course of action was right; I had no choice; I felt I was surviving . . . but how do I survive the guilt, and worse, the *shame* . . . ?"

This 23-year-old woman left therapy after 6 months to pursue a much beloved career in another city. I was young, too, in a young profession, eager to learn. I was very attached to her, and confused by her departure so soon after therapy began. I felt that therapy was a positive experience for her yet I was not able to pinpoint exactly why. I asked her if she could tell me how, if at all, I was of any help to her. She said, with a matter-of-fact voice that only the young are capable of: *"You understand me. You could listen to what bothered me."*

She left me bothered: Is that all? Understanding, listening, priest hearing confession? What about interpretations; archaeological diggings to uncover mystery, enlightenment, and reconstruction; what about reflections and cognitive restructuring? Iris challenged my professional persona by pointing out my personhood.

Using Iris' case as a prototype, I came to realize that who and what I was with them made the difference—that people are yearning for understanding, love, and warmth, genuineness, acceptance, and nonpossessiveness (cf. previous chapter). These qualities, I should reemphasize, all stem from the person therapist. With such a person clients feel at ease and trusting, able to voice (i.e., to define and determine) what it is that bothers one about their feelings, thoughts, and fantasies, and to regain a sense of autonomy and self-esteem. And the person client is more easily guided toward this aim, due to meeting a real, tangible person therapist. Paradoxically, change might ensue when one is not expected to change.

Rogers (1961) viewed therapy generally along these lines. He stated:

> If the therapy were optimal, intensive as well as extensive, then it would mean that the therapist has been able to enter into an intensely personal and subjective relationship with the client—relating not as a scientist to an object of study, not as a physician expecting to diagnose and cure, but as a person to a person. It would mean that the therapist feels this client to be a person of unconditional self-worth: of value no matter what his condition,

his behavior, or his feelings. It would mean the feelings which organically he is experiencing. It would mean that the therapist is able to let himself go in understanding this client; that no inner barriers keep him from sensing what it feels like to be the client at each moment of the relationship; and that he can convey something of his emphatic understanding to the client. (pp. 184–185)

In his writings Rogers expanded on the nature of "empathic understanding." For him empathy, acceptance, and the therapist's genuineness, are at the core of therapeutic change. Empathy—that sensitivity of a person which is not in the service of narcissistic needs—entails experiencing. And when one is open to the experiential field; when one is open to feelings toward another, then one does not employ superficial, impersonal superstructures such as countertransference. One is actively involved in an "intensely personal and subjective relationship." The psychobiographic approach to psychotherapy is *interactive,* which means that the person therapist is present not only, or mainly, with empathy, and empathic understanding, but also with his or her own biography, past and present.

After reading many of Rogers' writings and listening to his recordings, I am impressed that he holds an indecisive position regarding the therapist's self-disclosure. In 1957, he says: "Certainly the aim is not for the therapist to express or talk out his own feelings, but primarily that he should not be deceiving the client as to himself" (p. 98). He acknowledges that at times a therapist may need to talk out some of his own feelings. We are not talking about discussing how I feel the client is feeling, which is actually a reflection of feelings, the main avenue by which a client-centered therapist converses with the other party. The issue is personal feelings, and more; personal, biographical, real events. I remind the reader that therapy is about disclosing to another deep feelings, thoughts, and cravings.

Therapy would be meaningless if there were no interpretation of real events in life, for the sake of understanding their meaning(s) for the developing person. Here I refer to biographical interpretations, which are totally different from psychodynamic interpretations aimed at uncovering the contents of the unconscious. Biographical interpretation is time-tethered, it is historical, and it aims at pointing out possible multidimensional scripts of development of personality (inner reality, or self), vocational interests, interpersonal styles and needs, etc.

Genuineness, then, is more than being "accurately himself in this hour of this relationship" (Rogers, 1957, p. 97), and more than expressing one's own feelings about how the other person feels, it is being there genuinely as a human being who has feelings, and a biography. Through reciprocal self-disclosing, therapy becomes a real meeting, a giving and taking process.

A word of warning: there was a time when I witnessed how some therapists lose their boundaries, taking the other person to their home, sort of "adopting" the other person, while others in an uninhibited fashion "disclose" their intimate life out of their own narcissistic needs—at such times I doubted self-disclosure, only to realize later that there is no need to throw the baby out with the bathwater. In part III on "psychobiographic psychotherapy," I will delineate conditions of therapeutic biographical self-disclosure, based on the principles outlined in the above chapters.

CHAPTER TWELVE

The Objectives of Psychobiographic Psychotherapy

Here I refer to "aiming at making sense of a person's unique life history" in our definition of psychotherapy.

The reader may notice that it is a positive definition in the sense of an absence of theoretical conceptions of personality, and more importantly, an absence of pathological conceptions of personality development. Usually, theory dictates the goals of therapy. Thus, in Freudian theory the goal is redistribution of libidinal energy within the psychic apparatus, aiming toward genital maturity. In neo-Freudian object-relations theory, the goal is correction of characterologic distortions acquired through interpersonal events, aiming toward self-actualization and enhanced self-image. In social-learning theory the aim is extinction of faulty and destructive patterns of learning, aiming toward new and adaptive behaviors. According to the view expressed in this book, these goals are a manifestation of the power structure of psychotherapy claiming an authoritarian role of knowing what the norms and standards are, and imposing these theoretical, or at best statistical, artificial constructs on a living person.

Accordingly, the reader may also notice the absence of the notion of "cure," in the absolute or relative sense. Since we live in a sick society, we are all afflicted and wounded and oppressed by society's ills, and therefore the notion of "mental health" resonates a cultural idealization. This notion represents massive denial and ignorance of our fragile sociopolitical reality promulgated by either an intellectual or an economic elite, or both. "Mental health" is a class–cultural definition (i.e., it is an interpretation—that is, mental health that my culture says is mental health); it is a myth—unless personally defined. I might say that a developing sense of mental health "from its lower median is 'we,' and from its upper median, 'I.' "

Current psychological systems aim at modifying a person's distorted and unrealistic self-images (i.e., personal myths). The psychobiographic approach to psychotherapy also aims at the other "median": how class and cultural myths, or culture's sense of reality, blend with personal myths, or a person's sense of reality, affecting the evolving personality. In other words, psychobiographic psychotherapy aims to help the person to recognize the current and foregoing, that is, historical, social dilemmas, values, attitudes, actions, and myths in his or her own experience.

As an example, let us pose a question: what are we geared for in our evolution? Satisfaction? Pleasure? Self-actualization? A higher level of consciousness? Of course, historical era and class affiliation play a definitive role in determining which factor gets precedence, and in what manner. In general, the human race, at least in the Western Hemisphere, adheres to the belief that "life" should provide us not only with food and shelter but also with pleasure and satisfaction, in a broad sense, along with some sort of self-actualization. There is an immanent belief that the world, the Western world in our case, is geared toward this end of constant supply of provisions for human well-being in terms of material, intellectual, emotional, and instinctual fulfillment, that there is some order, though invisible, that takes care of that. We, fathers and mothers collaborating with our institutions, raise our children upon and with this belief.

What happens in the private, intimate world of the single individual whose illusion has been shattered by a world geared to sheer survival? What happens when that person comes to realize through hard-headed, rational intelligence, that the story of enlightenment, the story of individualism, the story of achievement through arduous competitive work, the story that if one is good and concentrates on one's task, one will ultimately be recognized (Novak, 1970)—that all are myths; that "success" is a matter of mere chance, personal connections, or market trends. There is nobody who takes care of his or her fellow human being. There is chaos, not order, in which one is a potential "disposable worker"(Castro, 1993).

Now, one can guess how our hypothetical individual feels: disappointment, rage over being deceived, and variable degrees of helplessness. This person is in conflict, yet it has nothing in common with psychodynamic notions of conflict; because, though feeling in distress, this person's perception, nevertheless, is accurate and realistic; there is a sensed discrepancy within the value system on which the person was raised, and the emotional reaction upon disillusionment, though appropriate in essence, might become self-defeating. This individual needs somebody's help in order to put into words these vague but accurate sensual perceptions; somebody to "be" with, for understanding and support, in order to transform this internal protest from self or the immediate environment into social action.

The goals of the psychobiographic approach to psychotherapy, then, are twofold: on the one hand, replacement of personal idealizations, or myths, with developmentally more appropriate self-images, and on the other hand, exposing the person to the interaction of self-idealization with cultural myths. The transformation of image of self, others, and events into words is the basic work of psychotherapy.

The suffering of individuals is embedded in a historical and political context. Underlying processes, latent conditions, and events, of which people at the time of their development—we speak of development per se after the fact—are partially or wholly unaware, and which set the boundaries of our existence—require an intentional backward gaze for sense to be made. A psychobiographic psychotherapy viewing a person as a living history, embedded in time and place, is attentive to such underlying processes as demographic shifts, work and market conditions, income distribution, and living arrangements. It aims at helping the individual integrate such confining events into a life history-story. The reader may notice the absence of the concept of selfhood, a psychological construct per se. Psychobiography denotes that a self has a biography, that self is a psychohistorical construct.

The parties are not geared as much toward understanding the events themselves, like their meaning for the history of the family which is a historical task per se, as toward understanding the personal subjective meaning of events and their effect on the development and formation of a personal world view. Psychological

trauma is a characteristic confining event demonstrating that an individual's sufferings are in continuous
interaction with historical and political processes. These
processes determine not only how we perceive some realities, but also how we handle them. Herman (1992)
writes:

> The systematic study of psychological trauma therefore
> depends on the support of a political movement. Indeed,
> whether such study can be pursued or discussed in public
> is itself a political question. The study of war trauma be-
> comes legitimate only in a context that challenges the
> sacrifice of young men in war. The study of trauma in
> sexual and domestic life becomes legitimate only in a
> context that challenges the subordination of women and
> children. Advances in the field occur only when they are
> supported by a political movement powerful enough to
> legitimate an alliance between investigators and patients
> and to counteract the ordinary social processes of silenc-
> ing and denial. (p. 9)

The psychobiographic approach aims at: (1) "making sense"—trying to discern the central underlying
story, or stories, that animate any particular person's life
(see McAdams, 1988). By definition, "making sense"
renders possibilities for dissolving helplessness; (2) The
terms *history* and *biography* denote a focus on the process, that "the person is a process, rather than a fixed set
of habits" (Rogers, 1980, p. 346), or an accumulation of
unrelated arbitrary events. What is transformed with a
well-narrated biography is the realization that though
one's life course has been defined by "unique" underlying patterns, one is always in process, always changing;
one is a "process person" (Rogers, 1980, p. 351).

Therapy is a process. The aims change as therapy
progresses, or regresses. The definition of aims on an

ongoing basis and then the definition of the means to that end—this is the act of therapy, as well as life. And it is a mutual act between two living persons in interaction.

PART III

PSYCHOBIOGRAPHIC PSYCHOTHERAPY

Preface: The Objectifying Processes and Dissociative Forces

> Our memory is fragile. Our lifetime
> is very brief; everything happens so
> fast that we have no time to un-
> derstand the relationship between
> events. . . .   (Allende, 1985)

Isabel Allende asserts, in the opening of *The House of the Spirits,* that "we write diaries in order to keep track of time." In the same vein, the psychobiographic approach asserts that people seek therapy because they want to keep track of themselves over time. Everything indeed happens so fast, too fast. With a blink of an eye we are no longer children, and with another, no longer adolescents. Soon we are facing sunset and death. We are moved from place to place. One day we are on one side of the ocean surrounded by people similar to us, uttering familiar words, and a few hours later, thanks to a flying box, we are on the other side of the ocean, surrounded, to our amazement and shock, by seemingly similar people uttering unintelligible words. We move from a beloved neighborhood to an unfamiliar one; from the country to the city; and from one city or country to another—nothing is permanent, fixed, secure. People come and go; some vanish on the battlefields of the megacities or the vast deserts and jungles of those seemingly similar people uttering unintelligible words.

Others inhabit a deep, dark, dense, remonstrating cloud of human ash above us. They are alive in their spirit. "Are you there—below—alive?" they are asking.

At first we try to relate to people; then we give up. Why should we try to relate to someone if that person is temporary, leaving soon, either physically or emotionally? Our childhood knights soon turn out to be ordinary pedestrians, many of them wracked with alcoholism, cancer, ego inflation, or a slew of other mundane conditions. The once loving father who absorbed my soul, conferring on it security, concern, and love, has now become my "lover" aiming at absorbing my body. The once loving mother of my brother who was first born, is now overwrought, dreamless, and helpless with me. Two, mom and dad, was once a magical number, a changeproof one. Nowadays, millions are familiar with the confusion-prone 0, 1, 3, 4 numbers.

Suddenly we may have two sets of parents, or one additional stepfather or stepmother. Millions are born into fatherless households, many of them to a mother with zero parenting skills because that is what a 14- or 16-year-old mother naturally can offer. Foster care has become an integral institution of a business-oriented era. And, as if all these forces of disintegration, whether human made or environmental, were not enough, one discovers that even the other institutions that assume the role of benefactors or protectors, such as the political system along with its systems of education, economics, mores, and morals, which dictates the structure of feeling of the postindustrialism era, are all geared toward loosening the relationships, the associations, between events, between persons, and between events and persons. Life as a meaningful process is antithetical to a life whose meaning is derived from purchase. In order to promulgate a belief that you are the car you drive, that self-determination is a matter of becoming Mr. Lambourgini, with a Rolex and Gucci accessories—you need dissociated individuals, who themselves were treated as objects, and who, in turn treat others, themselves among them, as objects. Objects, to refresh your memory, entail a process of transformation and control (i.e., exertion of power).

A plant becomes objectified by being cut, its flowers decorating our homes, or by being fertilized as long as it flowers, and then abandoned. Or it can be transformed from its natural environment and become an indoor plant to satisfy our quest for beauty. In order to have a chair to be used whenever I wish not to stand, I have to cut down a tree, using it as a material to be molded and transformed to a four-legged object. Now, imagine what might happen when the same material is used frequently, again and again, by being transformed and molded first into a chair, then into a desk, then into a ladder, and then into wooden spoons, and so on to the end when that erect tree has become sawdust. What would happen if a carpenter was available to the sawdust? Would it shout, "Transform me back to what I was"? What was it? A chair or a tree? But would it avail itself to the carpenter? Isn't the carpenter an expert in using the same tools that initiated and then perpetuated the tree's misery of being transformed from one object to another?

We are all exposed to the objectifying process. It is a human, but not humane, experience. Each of us is subjected to massive processes of standardization of individual thought and action into fixed mass patterns. Soren Kierkegaard (1938), from an idealistic point of view, warns us of this tendency to view the human person as an object, which has become accentuated with the coming of the industrial revolution and mass production, when he says: "The crowd is composed of individuals, but it must also be in the power of each one to be what he is: an individual; and no one, no one at all, no one whatsoever is prevented from being an individual unless he prevents himself—by becoming one of the masses . . ." (p. 179)

Nature contributes its share in objectifying the planet's inhabitants. Diseases such as cancer, for example, painfully expose the individual to being merely transient. The cancerous cell is indifferent, like its social counterparts, to one's personal, intimate feelings and thoughts, leveling one down to a mere thing.

Paradoxically, survival entails dissociation. But when dissociative processes are massively utilized as a consequence of massive objectifying processes, we encounter a person in psychological distress. In this sense humanity is traumatized. We are all implicated in this state of affairs of being objectified. As already emphasized, this context is decisive for the practice of psychotherapy.

Davis and Frawley (1994), to my view, took upon themselves the task of humanizing this phenomenon. This is how they define dissociation:

> Dissociation is the process of severing connections between categories of mental events—between events that seem irreconcilably different, between the actual events and their affective and emotional significance, between actual events and the awareness of their cognitive significance, and finally, as in the case of severe trauma, between the actual occurrence of real events and their permanent, symbolic, verbal mental representation. (p. 42)

Revival of the dissociated is at the core of the psycho-biographic therapeutic endeavor. I have suggested that in order to dissociate the dissociated, one must refrain from utilizing the same means and processes that produced the dissociations in the first place. In other words, technical means and objectifying processes perpetuate what they allege to cure. These "techniques" are inherent in the nonegalitarian and dehumanized systems of psychotherapy based upon dehumanized notions of human suffering, that are converted into scientific systems of abnormal psychology.

Let me remark immediately that the agent of this process of revival of the dissociated is not the alleged professional "knower." The psychobiographer, or the psychotherapist in the traditional sense, is, or should be, the knower of his or her own dissociates and objectifying processes. The therapist should be the owner of his or her own psychobiography. A dissociated person therapist whose personal emotional–intellectual–social–economical history is in a state of loose, vague, and fragmented relationships, whose body is dissociated from the brain, whose head is dissociated from the heart, and the brain from the genitals, the outer from the inner—this therapist is a thing, a behaving thing, and as such resembles the carpenter who is asked to transform the chair to the original tree. The therapist is helpless, and even though in possession of impressive tools, he or she is actually capable of no more than mere gluing and nailing. The therapist holds no transforming capabilities as a thing but only as an experiencing person. The therapist experiences as well as behaves. By *revival of the dissociated,* then, I mean that the psychobio-graphic approach is geared toward making the encounter an *experience.* In order to get back to experience, to the dissociated experience, in order to reexperience and approximate the actual and real reality, one must dedissociate, and dedepersonalize, and deobjectify. Psychotherapy is the craft of helping people experience what they already know. I will expand on this key concept later.

CHAPTER THIRTEEN

The Psychobiographic Approach and Developmental Psychology

Almost every school of thought acknowledges that early childhood experiences are of crucial importance for the individual as well as for society as a whole, through the actions of the individuals. Schools differ in the extent of compensatory factors they attribute to maturational processes. Thus, according to object relational theories, subsequent compensatory factors have little impact on the later development of a morbid personality whose foundations have been melted down during these early years. On the other hand, learning theories give full attribution to these same compensatory factors for the later personality development to the extent of abolition of early childhood experiences. And one wonders: why the logos of psyche insists on fragmentation of experience, of time, especially when our concern is the applied science of the psyche? Thus, one therapist is focusing on the analysis of transference neurosis in order to help the patient gain access to unconscious repressed childhood conflicts, and another therapist, dwelling as if in another galaxy, is geared toward reconditioning the patient's current behavior. Both therapists may actually be living in the same neighborhood, even on the same street, yet in terms of time they live billions of moments apart.

159

To what extent life is undetermined is illustrated by the fact that you, the prospective client, whose sense of time is actually at stake, as implied by the concept of dissociation—may enter the door of this or that time machine just by chance! "The link between time and reality is insoluble" says Mann (1973). "We can divorce ourselves from time only by undoing reality, or from reality only by undoing the sense of time. Categorical time is measured by clocks and calendars; existential time is that which is experienced, lived in, rather than observed" (p. 3).

St. Augustine called a person's present the memory of things past and the expectation of things to come. This existential, subjective meaning of time is, as Mann contends, an inseparable element of time. Every life history, therefore, and every human behavior is linked with time as a united and unifying agent. An *I–thou* relationship can be made possible only when there is conscious effort by the partner to approximate the Other's time agency.

One disables real meeting (and meaning), introduces coercion, creates further alienation, and enhances psychopathology by perpetuating it, while one is engaged in projecting into the Other a sense of time, which derives its legitimacy and its potency from a predisposed theoretical time, as practiced in current systems of psychotherapy. In the psychobiographic approach, and in therapy in general, in my view, this approximation is the function of the psychobiographer, by being fully attentive to the Other's biographical time. Biographical time is a conceptualized existential time; or it is a subjective, yet event-related, sense of time. A biographical time derives its potency and reality from the person's unique past–current–future life history. A person is sitting shivering in front of me. He is coming from home. And he is scared. I wonder if anything disturbing happened at home or on his way to the clinic—*present time*. Maybe something in me is disturbing him—*present time*. And maybe this thing in me is actually a reminder of something far back related to grandfather? Father? Teacher? Stranger?—*past time*. What about something in between us, say fear of the void, death—*timelessness*. Or, maybe he is trembling while anticipating his future or that of someone dear to him—*future time*. Or maybe he just has a fever!—*present time*.

It is quite obvious how a therapist with a specific theoretical or personal time preference will be directed by their own sense of time, or their construct of time agency, and will proceed with inquiries and interpretations of repressed memories or irrational beliefs. The present state of trembling might indeed have some roots in the past, as anybody may have had some sort of disturbing encounter with some disturbing people, including fathers and mothers, and, as is known in the realm of the metaphysical, one may find whatever one's heart desires. This kind of inquiry will lead to something which is true but not real. On the other hand, one may be geared to the here-and-now construct of time agency, and may be able to be empathically and genuinely with the Other's existential sense of trembling present time. This is definitely a real experience of time. Yet, in order to be also true, it must be linked to a biographical piece, to something that actually happened. It must have an historical underpinning, which includes contemporary history, the present, but is not limited to it. Then we can speak about reality.

Trauma is a biographical event which contains an historical truth, and as such it has relevance for psycho-therapeutic inquiry; whereas fantasy and a belief only maintain a potentiality when linked to an event, and that event, I may remind the reader, might be of any kind, including, but not limited to, an event of oedipal origin. People in therapy are struggling with living, with the experience of living, or, in short, with experience. Their experience of time has been dissociated and frag-mented to the degree that time has lost its property as a continuous, unified, and unifying experience. The problem of experience, in life as well as in the life of therapy, is how to live in the present with the memories of the past and the anticipation of the future.

How dissociated and depersonalized biographical pieces of time are being revived in a psychobiographic approach to psychotherapy is the subject of the present chapter. But first let me connect us to a period in our development which has left no traceable history because it was characterized by timelessness (i.e., time as a con-tinuous whole) and, as I will show, by something else of crucial importance.

I am referring to the postnatal embryonic phase of development in which the child is still contained within its mother though its body is already born. In this phase, says Neumann (1973), there is a primary unity of mother and child. The child gradually emerges from this unity to become an individual subject confronting the world as thou and as object. For the child in this phase, continues Neumann, the mother is neither out-side nor inside; and it, the child, does not experience her breasts as alien and outside. "As in the uterine phase, child and mother are still so *intermeshed* as to be one; they form a dual union" (Neumann, 1973, p. 12;

emphasis added). For Neumann, who is strongly affiliated with the Jungian system of psychology, this dual union of the primal relationship is cosmic and transpersonal in nature.

Indeed, the mother is neither outside nor inside, as Neumann argues. She is there. The child, indeed, does not experience her breast as alien and outside. The infant experiences it as friendly, as alimentary, and as being there to meet all needs. This union is an archetype, though not in a Jungian sense, of the union between me and you, I–thou, the psychobiographer and the autobiographer. The psychobiographer is there, demarcated as the mother's primary bodily existence. I will continue to argue that a psychobiographer who is there as a real person (i.e., with a clearly defined personal biography) will enhance a dual union, by creating an alimentary symbiosis which is decisive for personal emotional growth. When one is clear, "known" to another, then the interpersonal space is free of redundant noise and contamination and open for mutual exploration, as well as—and this is so important—for self-explorations. Alimentary symbiosis is more a meeting than a merging, though at some point in the process of this specific kind of meeting, the meeting will take the form of a union, strongly so by and for the Other.

Person after person has confirmed what Alma had to say at our separation session. She was in her 40s, struggling with deep depression after divorcing an extremely violent alcoholic husband. She was also grieving over her beloved deceased father and a dog, and one of her children had been diagnosed as having cancer. I asked this woman what, if anything, I had given her during the year she came to me. She said with no hesitation that what she liked the most was "that you were obvious. No mystery about you. You let me know you, you know what I mean, as a human being; I could ask you questions, even personal ones . . . and you were at ease with this. . . . After a while I was not anymore bothered with you, you know, who you are, what you are, what you really think about me. I was engaged entirely with myself.''

Relying on personal history (i.e., psychobiography), I had many so-called supervisors of many kinds. Some types of them might shed some light on the correct interpretation of Alma's disclosure and the issue of the psychobiographer's demarcation. All these supervisors, of course, treated me as they treated their patients. One type was the business-oriented kind: you bring material and I "help" you to cast meaning into it by analyzing, or discussing if you prefer, why you said what you said when you said it. I put "help" in quotation marks because actually it was "I show you," as might be expected from an expert-oriented convention (see previous chapters). This type of supervising therapist was very much "interested" in my patient's (and my) so-called transferential reactions. We—I and my patient through me—were expected to disclose whatever and whenever we were asked, for the sake of "learning," for me, and "emotional health," for the patient.

I met with such a type once a week for a whole year. Except for his physical appearance, his dressed body, I knew only that he owned an old brown Volvo. I did not get involved in gossip that conceals the truth more than reveals it, and certainly serves the goal of idealizing the person of the therapist. I could not openly question the one-sided intrusions and risk the accusation of resistance. In fact, I did so a few times but I was so misunderstood (i.e., misinterpreted) that I quickly learned that if I wanted to achieve my goal of graduating from that institute, or, in other words, if I did not want to incriminate myself, and at the same time if I wanted somehow to keep my self-respect and self-esteem intact, I should in such a unilateral situation resort to tactics of some sort. Certainly, I did not want to be labeled a neurotic if neurosis is defined as telling the right thing to the wrong person.

Alma was confronted with the same dilemma. She went through a severe emotional adversity after she was forced to take her four children and flee empty-handed from the above-mentioned abusive husband. This husband had hit her, threatened her and her children constantly, and stalked and followed her for 14 years. Her father, a weak person yet her sole soulmate, and her young brother had both died a few years before her flight. Her mother, who was deeply attached to her deceased son to the extent of ignoring Alma, had no real ability or will to support her. In the face of such massive objectifying processes Alma became depressed and delusional. She lost her compass, literally losing direction a few times while on her way to or from home. When things had reached an impasse, she was taken by her mother to a psychiatrist. Alma could relate to what she called "that horrifying event" only months after her therapy with me began. "I was so scared. I was afraid he was going to say I was mad and hospitalize me. How could I tell him I felt that he [her husband] was everywhere following me, that I had hallucinations [of being instructed by a man to do things]. . . . I didn't want to incriminate myself. . . . When he asked me all those testing questions I wanted to shout at him, 'how would *he* feel if . . .' but I was too weak, and anyway I didn't want to make things worse." She decided to opt for sanity—by not saying the right things.

Returning to me and the expert supervisor therapist, I made a very correct judgment that a discourse would be impossible, and because I had no intention, for all the reasons I delineated in this work, to let myself and my "patients" be analyzed or treated by any theory or quasi-theory about human suffering and existence, I ventured to teach the "expert" a lesson in the real logos of the psyche. At times I invested all my personal and theoretical knowledge in the cases I brought with me to the supervisory sessions. I was so well prepared, and the case was presented so fluently, with such a passion and knowledge, that the "expert" had little to say and a lot to learn. At other times, when I was forced to absorb the other's knowledge, I just invented a whole therapy session out of my imagination. I knew so intimately my partner, my "patient," that intuitively I was able to invent a scenario. But, just as intuitively, I knew my supervisor, who was so transparent to me that I knew what he expected, what delighted him, and what made him believe we were "working." I made every effort to disconnect the assumed parallel processes between the supervisory sessions and the therapeutic sessions. I called this the process of unlearning, on which I will expand later. What really happened in the one had little in common with what happened in the other. One was saturated with mutuality, the other with power maneuvers.

A second type of supervisor-therapist I encountered used the professionally self-disclosing kind: you are invited to participate in an as-if personal relationship. This type holds to the conviction that by disclosing one's experiences in life, the therapist serves as a role model for imitation or identification, whereas the real underlying motif for such self-disclosures is either a narcissistic need for self-aggrandizement or an inability to endure the tension inherent in any interpersonal relationship. In this type the infantilizing and patronizing processes are at their height, though in the disguise of an apparently benevolent act.

In both cases the person is objectified in order to please an insecure expert and cover up his or her deficiencies as a human being. What I claim is that this practice, rather than being an exception, is the rule.

These cases, the one in which the therapist is an unidentified person therapist who does not relate to any personal biography, and the other in which the therapist is overpresent with his or her biography, both create an interpersonal atmosphere in which the other person is much too much engaged with the person of the therapist. Mystification, idealization, and interpersonal anxiety stand as buffers and impede the Other's (patient/client's) capacity for self-identity and self-definition. Both attitudes postulate a deficiency on the part of the other party while in fact it is either a projection on the part of the expert-therapist or a joint deficiency, or both. In these cases the interpersonal space is full of redundant noise and is contaminated with power used for control and not liberation.

The question is: What kind of psychobiographic disclosure liberates? The answer is, one in which the presence of one person resembles the presence of the mother as just being there and providing the Other with what psychological food the Other needs. The specific ingredients of this psychobiographic demarcation, which constitutes an important facet of the I–thou

relationship I called primary alimentary symbiosis, constitutes the subject of the following chapters. At this
point I wish to specify another property of the primary
alimentary symbiosis.

As mentioned above, there was a period in our development which has left no traceable history in the mind
of the individual because it was characterized by timelessness and by something else of crucial importance:
powerlessness. The object relational theories of human
psychic development—Freud's oral phase, Mahler's
(Mahler, Pine, & Bergman, 1975) subphases of the
separation-individuation process, Klein's paranoid-
depressive position (Segal, 1964)—attribute to this early
phase of human development a feeling of total power
that is accountable for the infantile magical attitude toward the world. In fact, this early pre-ego phase, Neumann (1973) contends, is characterized by an absence
of differentiation between world, mother, and self-body,
and hence it is characterized by lack of power. "It is
meaningful to speak of power," says Neumann, "only
when an ego is present whose libido charge, or will, is
strong enough to desire and exert power, and to empower itself of an object" (p. 47). None of these theories applies to the subjectless and objectless postnatal
embryonic phase of development in which the child is
still contained within its mother, though its body has
already been born.

The primary unity of mother and child is not of an
autistic nature. Self-affirmation, an affirmative attitude
toward oneself and one's personality, develops in the
course of the primal relationship, which is in a very
meaningful sense interpersonal (Neumann, 1973).

In the primal relationship, the experience of powerlessness takes the form of harmony with the mother,

and later with one's self and with nature at large. As noted earlier, massive violation of the sense of harmony by massive application of objectifying processes is demonstrable in all character and psychotic disorders. In a psychobiographic I–thou relationship, the Other goes through an emotionally satisfying experience of lack of power which in turn is experienced as security that stems from genuine and harmonious togetherness, and emotional concern and care. It provides an experience of shelteredness in the continuity of existence. The mother of the primal relationship was a "good enough" shelter yet anonymous and transpersonal; it means "good Great Mother," if one needs to follow Neumann's terminology. Accordingly, it is not the personal individual, but the generically maternal that is the indispensable foundation of the child's life (Neumann, 1973). In the psychobiographic approach, the psychobiographer is known and personal; in other words, he or she is archetypal, not in the Jungian sense but in the sense of being atypical of the postprimal relationships by providing the adult child with a shelter devoid of power dynamics which ultimately will empower the Other to marshall his or her compensatory processes that enable a meaningful dialectical relationship between an autonomous development and collectivity.

A clearly demarcated humane psychobiographer is the only "power" present in this encounter, and by being clear—and also, but not only, as Rogers noted, by being genuine—one is providing the Other in any kind of relationship with an interpersonal environment that facilitates growth and change. This, in my view, is the human meaning of the therapeutic relationship. It is also an antidote to the guruism and cultism so prevalent in psychotherapy which derive their potency from the

mysterious (anonymous), the idealized, and the roman-
ticized.

What is the nature of this growth? Age appropriate
individuation.

For Jung, and from a different perspective for Rank
(see especially 1936/1978, p. 2), individuation implies
rebirth, a psychological–spiritual rebirth or recreation.
In his later life and thinking Jung receded totally from
historicism, from personal history, and dived deeper
and deeper into what is "beyond" scientific psychology,
beyond the personal into the transpersonal and the collective archetypal unconscious. As early as circa 1912,
Jung (1912/1991) writes that "the supposition is justified that ontogenesis corresponds in psychology to phy-
logenesis. Consequently, it would be true, as well, that
the state of infantile thinking in the child's psychic life,
as well as in dreams, is nothing but a re-echo of the
*pre*historic and the ancient" (p. 25). Jungian psychoanalysis, from my vantage point of the inherent power
structure of psychotherapy, resembles in every aspect
Freudian psychoanalysis and other cognito-behavioral
analyses. Some aspects of these rebirth (i.e., redemption, individuation) theories in psychology need to be
addressed as they are often understated. These aspects
reflect on the dangers of these ahistorical methods in
psychotherapy, as well as some of their usages.

Jung repeatedly reminded his readers that we are all
born within a specific historical context and that this
fact gives form to the specific conflicts played out in the
individual psyche. Jung, then, as Noll (1994) says, would
agree with Weber's conviction that we are essentially
"historical beings"; so, asks Noll, who is the historical
Jung? And I might add another question: why did Jung
and his disciples withdraw from the historical to the

mythological; why is a person being equated with spirit (person = spirit)?

Noll's careful study is another proof of the inseparable interaction between a person and the cognitoemotional categories of his or her cultural era. He reconstructs the intellectual currents of *fin de siècle* Germany that influenced Jung. The notions of race and power, extrapolated from Nietzsche's thought, played a central role within the intellectual circles at the turn of the century. Nietzsche fantasized the creation of a "New Man" and a "new nobility" or a new elite that would revolutionize human culture and lead it to a new utopia. This same fantasy is one of the many mystical or prefascist sources of National Socialism. Noll believes that the term *spiritual elitism* is more appropriate to these cults than cultural elitism.

Freud's and Jung's notions were among the most prominent spiritual elites of this kind in German Europe during the period from 1890 to 1933. Both are highly subjective, based on acquiring some faculty through analysis and on the authority of the analyst to interpret a mysterious realm of human experience. Both are social organizations around persons who claim to have special abilities, which set them apart from others, developed only through a defined "extraordinary experience" (i.e., personal analysis) and quickly became aristocratic elites with primarily self-serving economic and political agendas (see Noll, 1994, pp. 54–56). Noll continues: "Jung's later claim for individuation (rebirth) through analysis (initiation) may be rooted in the same *fin de siècle* fantasy, one of a society influenced by a few perpetually creative, individuated human beings" (p. 57). Noll sees Jung's break with Freud in 1912 not as a split within the psychoanalytic movement but as Jung's turning away from science and his founding of a new religion, which offered a rebirth (i.e., "individuation"), like the one celebrated in ancient mystery cult teachings. Jung consciously inaugurated a cult of personality centered on himself and passed down to the present by a body of priest-analysts.

Earlier I proposed that, like us, the mental health practitioners, as well as those who seek our services, Jung was attracted to psychiatry because of his own personal–emotional deprivations; that he hoped to find a way to overcome his own personality problems, especially in the light of his own heredity. It has also been proposed that there are as many personality theories as there are people, though in terms of common denominators they can be clustered into several hundreds. Jung *had* to break from the historically oriented (e.g., repressed memories of childhood) Freud. He needed a personal *religion* because he had no interest in personal history and "historical beings." Jung's memories of his own childhood were not repressed but alive and painful, too painful. From very early days he had been exposed to what I call massive objectifying processes by his emotionally disordered and depressive mother and an irritable and difficult-to-get-along-with father. He found positive relatedness only with a piece of wood (a manikin) in the shelter of an attic. He did not show much interest in people throughout his life, just as his primary people had not shown interest in him.

One of Jung's closest disciples in his last decades said about him: "When you met him in [the Psychological Club] or when you met him privately or *in analysis,* it was always a man interested in the, I would like to use the word, in the *spiritual* food. Always. And to the depths" (cited in Noll, 1994, p. 18; emphasis added).

In other words, Jung was not interested in you, but rather in your spirit. The spirit is a part of but not the whole person; this is another reflection of objectifying a human being in therapy. Jung himself was never interested in the laborious, painstaking act of therapy, and did not practice therapy to a meaningful extent. Yet he made therapy what it never had been: an extrabiographical, non-interpersonal-relational, spiritual–religious experience.

The personal, as opposed to the transpersonal, aims at differentiating "fact" from fantasy. The analysis of the transpersonal, through dream symbolism, aims at implementing fantasy for those whose personal lives have been too much to bear, who need a transpersonal spiritual figure or figures to substitute for the felt absence of a personal psychohistorical figure. This kind of "individuation," or spiritual rebirth, might be of use for those people who were not, and will not be able to be, in what I call alimentary symbiosis. They cannot connect, relate, or bond except on a spiritual level. Therapy was not and should not be a cult related, or cultlike, religious experience if only for the mundane reason that thousands and at times hundreds of thousands of dollars are involved in these kinds of therapies which, as was noted earlier, perpetuate one's misery. Perpetuation of human misery is at the root of any aristocratic elite with primarily self-serving economic and political agendas. Psychotherapy as cult is a sham, a very expensive one, materially and emotionally (= "spiritually").

The following is an example of what the ahistorical rebirth cults in psychotherapy can lead to. The author, described as a "Zurich-trained Jungian analyst in private practice," in a chapter entitled "The Provisional Personality," has the following to say about mid-life:

> The transit of the Middle Passage occurs in the fearsome clash between the acquired personality and the demands of the Self. A person going through such an experience will often panic and say, "I don't know who I am anymore." In effect, the person one has been is to be replaced by the person to be. *The first must die.* No wonder there is such enormous anxiety. One is summoned, psychologically, to die unto the old self so that the new might be born.
>
> Such death and rebirth is not an end in itself; it is a passage. It is necessary to go through the Middle Passage to more nearly achieve one's potential and to earn the vitality and wisdom of mature aging. Thus, the Middle Passage represents a summons from within to move from the provisional life to true adulthood, from the false self to authenticity. (Hollis, 1993, p. 15; emphasis added)

The self here is endowed with religious properties. It can easily be replaced by "the demands of" Jesus, God, Moses, Buddha (and the indoctrinations of the analyst). It is not an integrating–organizing entity in and of the personality as in, for example, the Rogerian self psychology, but a destructive–annihilating entity that is not subject to, and is not governed by, the personality, by the person him or herself. It is an emissary on a mission, the mission being the assassination of four decades of life, more than half of an average life's duration; it is a systematic method of extermination of historicism, of personal history, of a person's biography and psychobiography. "The Middle Passage starts," says the author, "when we ask, 'Who am I, *apart* from my history and the roles I have played?'" (Hollis, 1993, p. 19; emphasis added). It aims at replacing "facts," "truths," and personal myths with spiritual mythology. Life is not viewed as a developing process with a sequence, but as a deteriorating process which leads ultimately to enlightenment, if only you choose the right psychological church. As such, life is a process entailing detachment (i.e., emotional/spiritual death of the old); in other words, life, according to the rebirth cult, entails ("summons") dissociation. Negation of the past is accomplished. The person-to-person is replaced by person-to-cosmos (through the mediation of the analyst, of course). Here we have another illustration of perpetuation of human misery under the guise of psychotherapy.

Individuation, then, does not imply rebirth. The pain of living itself is too taxing to invite another birth. Like Rank, whose last book was entitled *Beyond Psychology*, Rogers concluded, by the end of his life, after practicing psychotherapy for half a century, that there is a realm (a reality or realities) "beyond" scientific psychology, and he spoke of it in terms such as "the transcendent, the indescribable, the spiritual" (Thorne, as cited in Kramer, 1995). What then is the spiritual dimension of living as manifested in psychotherapy, as opposed to its manifestation in cultism?

"Ironically," says Kramer (1995), "the spiritual had always been there, hidden in what was closest and most familiar to Rogers: the empathic relationship between therapist and client" (p. 54). Laing (1967) agrees that scientific psychology should study the regularities pervading the sequence, rhythm, and tempo of the therapeutic situation and process, but he acknowledges that "the really decisive moments in psychotherapy, as every patient or therapist who has ever experienced them knows, are unpredictable, unique, unforgettable, always unrepeatable, and often indescribable" (p. 47). Does this mean that psychotherapy must be a pseudo-esoteric cult, asks Laing? "No," he answers; we must continue to struggle through our confusions and insist on being human. "Psychotherapy must remain an obstinate attempt of two people to recover the wholeness of being human through the relationship between them. . . . And any *theory* not founded on the nature of being human is a lie and betrayal of man" (Laing, 1967, p. 45). Laing, Rogers, and Rank predicate the spiritual dimension of psychotherapy on the experience of relationship between human beings in interaction. The focus is on experience as well as transaction: how we transact or interact with each other as well as how we experience each other. Human beings everywhere, including those in psychotherapy, are able to live in the spirit only, and only, by deep sharing.

In life, as well as in psychotherapy, to live in the spirit entails more than empathic union between I and thou. Deep sharing, real intimacy (i.e., alimentary symbiosis), entails exchange of personal historical events and experiences, intellectual as well as emotional—of psychobiography.

Individuation in the psychobiographic sense means: How am I, at this juncture of my life, with these memories of my past and these hopes for my future, how am I going to live in maximum autonomy (i.e., liberty) and in maximum collectivity? In maximum oneness and maximum difference? Liberation contains a vector of power. How much power am I going to exert for the sake of my perceived autonomy; to what extent am I going to objectify myself and others, or vice versa, to gratify my personal sense of competence, importance, and egoness. Individuation entails will and choice. Psychobiographic individuation relies heavily on developmental psychology and on sociohistorical developments; and it is always age appropriate.

The problem of individuation is reflected in the story of the attempted sacrifice of Isaac. God tells Abraham to take his only son and offer him as a burnt offering, and Abraham obeys (Genesis: 22). Which voice should one obey? Which voice can one afford to obey? This is still the central dilemma of human existence: Do I have the courage to listen to my internal voice and make my own decisions? If resorting to therapy is seen as protest, I would say that an individual comes to therapy because that person is not satisfied with the way this dilemma has been resolved in and by him or her.

CHAPTER FOURTEEN

The Process of Unlearning

A chapter on technique does not naturally belong in my writing. The concept of technique implies, among other things mentioned earlier, an adherence to a body of certain rules, and a deliberate attempt to achieve a perfection in execution precluding the humane dimensions (*ergo,* perfect). I have attempted to write about the spirit of a helping and humane relationship precluding technology. Such an approach implies individuality and creativity.

I have never had a format for the beginning of a meeting. No two meetings are the same, so that I never ask the same questions, and never prepare myself for a meeting. I am always curious to know who the Other really is, what brings the Other to where he or she is, and whether we will be able to make a meaningful contact. And I always, always, bring with me to any such meeting a sense of deep respect for a person in very specific distress who still is capable of again taking the risk of meeting yet another person. If charts and records are available I read them carefully, trying to depict the themas (Murray et al., 1938) around which the person's life has been organized, and that will help me to speculate about what sort of human interaction he or she might need. I look for organic factors if they are present, and for suicidal potential; and if there are no emergency issues which entail crisis intervention, I wait to

179

know a new person in my life, but also to let that person know me.

I know that inside, the person who sits across from me feels defeated by life. Every act of the initial phases of the meeting is aimed at addressing this issue that emanates from the common belief that only those who cannot cope with life due to some innate defects and weaknesses resort to psychotherapy. This aim is often communicated through acknowledgment of the Other's struggles in life and appraisal of achievements in spite of the obstacles that the person has confronted throughout the life cycle. The aim is conversion of the sense of defeat to a sense of hope, and eventually victory. I usually prefer the straightforward direct approach of asking very early, but not too early, before some exchange of ideas and information occurs:

How do you feel, coming here to psychotherapy, to me? Have any ideas crossed your mind?

Usually I get some general, noncommittal statements which reveal a little but conceal twice as much. The content at this stage is not of import by itself because I strive to deliver the message that I am aware and not in denial of this issue and that I encourage questioning even if it involves uncomfortable issues. If the answer does not avail itself for further and deeper explorations, I usually make a statement that addresses the sense and concept of defeat and not the feeling or feelings underlying the sense of defeat, such as shame. I do not want to empathize with the feeling, which at this stage is correctly felt, thereby reinforcing it, but to challenge it. Dysfunctional feelings—and by that I mean feelings that stem from external sources that have not yet gone through a self-examination and assimilation process—that are wrapped around a convention, will change with the abandonment of that convention and acquisition of a new set of self-chosen perceptions. The person, stimulated by questions, commences a long, personal, and at times interpersonal and intimate process of contemplation about, and unlearning of, previously held answers to the questions of life.

Did that person, who is the so-called patient, indeed content him or herself with "wrong answers to the questions of life," as Jung (1961) wrote in his autobiography, and as myriads of psychotherapists believe their prospective patients do? Of course, as I argue, these theorists, including Jung and other famous therapists, forget that this same "wrongness" was responsible for they themselves pursuing the mental health profession and going into their own psychotherapy or, if it sounds better, "analysis." Did Jung, as a typical example, know what the questions of life are? Would anybody dare say he or she knows? Of course, those who know what reality is would dare say so. Then, it might surprise you to hear me declare that "I know!" Yet I will immediately add that "at this point of my life I believe I know what the questions of life are for *me;* I am constantly searching for adequate answers which I know are temporary ones, always changing. It might turn out that I find the wrong answer, or even the wrong question, but then it is wrong later and not at the time of its occurrence, is wrong only ipso facto, and if so it was not wrong even when it is wrong."

This same "wrongness," I have come to understand, is responsible for the "patient's" resorting to therapy. If the person client is blamed for something he or she deep inside does not feel responsible for (at least in its origins), but has to believe it is correct (otherwise why go to psyche therapy) then no wonder that I, the therapist, am correctly perceived as an enemy, and the "patient" as a failure and defeated person. The very act of going to a therapist is an act of empowering the powerlessness. (The very reason for coming to therapy in the first place, I remind you, is the extreme feeling of helplessness in face of massive objectifying processes.) The perception of therapy as enemy, or as defeat, is not a "dysfunctional belief"; it is not a "cognitive distortion" or delusion or some sort of paranoid ideation. It is perfectly correct subjectively and objectively—it is real, it is reality. People are defeated by life events, and by oppressive conditions and circumstances; by poverty, by discrimination (racial, social, political, sexual, intrafamilial); by false sociopolitical, class–elitist oriented values such as materialism, narcissism, and hedonism; by crude abuse. People are defeated because they have been provided with the wrong answers to the questions of life. The act of coming to therapy paradoxically symbolizes an innate motivation for growth and an unspoken desire to provide different questions and therefore different answers to a lived life.

From the very beginning every motion, intonation, gesture, and statement aims at signaling respect for the basic fact that we are all simply human beings and as such we are equal in every respect; and though we are different, because of belonging to the human race we have many things in common to be explored and discovered. The Other is stirred to think more deeply about the common problems of life.

I do not have a couch, and my chair is of the same quality as the Other's. We as a society have abolished monarchism but only in form; its spirit remains alive, and displaced into worship of material idols and arti-facts. These include status symbols, and material, spiri-tual, and intellectual cults, or, more accurately, fashions, such as the cults of celebrities, whether Freudian, Jung-ian, political, or Hollywoodian. I remember how one of my first "supervisors," a young woman in her 30s, described to us neophytes with fervent eyes and hands thrown forward as in prayer, the gothic building which housed a psychoanalytic institute she visited, with its antique Victorian furniture and decoration. "Ah, so no-ble," she was saying. And I thought of the multitude, of psychotherapy being a mass movement. Indeed it is a mass movement; though trying to alienate itself from its objectives and ally itself with what is perceived as unique, noble, elite.

Office decor and atmosphere portray this separatist attitude. The furniture the expert uses is usually of a better quality than the "patient's"; the presence of many status symbols conveys a sense of class uniqueness; the lighting is arranged to deliver a special, deliberate message, ranging from holiness to an in-depth voyage into intimacy as if one had in mind a shrine, a personal bedroom, or a boudoir (with a bookshelf on the side).

Worst of all is "the lineage business." The monarchs and the nobles had to show lineage, and the further they could trace their family line into antiquity, the better regarded they were. The mental health practitioner's proof of lineage is the credentials displayed densely on an entire wall, preferably behind the therapist, but in front of the client's eyes—the more frames, the better. The more frames the therapist has that can be bought in any department store, the more knowledge he or she must have. The Other brings to the session a social be-lief prevalent in the Western hemisphere that quantity implies quality; that if one has a nice house (office) in a nice neighborhood ("You know, he lives where John Wayne lived"), with a dog, and a boat on the side lawn, if one has expensive attire and custom-made furniture, then that person must be successful. "I mean, this therapist has gotten so much money because he has so many people who come to him! Don't you think so? People wouldn't have come to him unless he was able to cure them, right? Then, he must be good. Look at his resume, he is the chairman of . . . director of . . . teacher at . . . member of . . . assistant professor at . . . he is so important!"

The purchasing cycle is on the run: the American Psychological Association, as well as other professional associations, mandates Continuing Education Credits and we indeed purchase credits but not necessarily knowledge. To buy knowledge and to acquire it are two different things. Vanity and knowledge dwell together as well as, and many times even better than, vanity and piling up goods. One of the least understood, and least accepted, phenomena of human existence is the fact that one might have a perfectly healthy mind in a perfectly sick soul. Unfortunately these sick souls very rarely come to therapy. They are perceived as perfectly normal (and moral) by others and by themselves. They have proofs of their normality; their credentials, a magna cum laude degree from a leading university, and emblems! (They are also those who start the world wars and other wars, and who create economic or political or personal slavery and the vast layers of poverty-ridden people.)

The Other comes to me with this purchasing mentality. At best, the Other wants knowledge in exchange for money. Once people exchanged flour seeds for

donkeys; nowadays we exchange pieces of paper (i.e.,
money) for morality, soul, or wisdom. And I refuse—from the outset!

Other: (as if engaging in self-talk) *Why does it happen*
      to me . . .?
Me: *Are you asking me or talking to yourself?*

    I make the utterance contextual–interpersonal. I
know that the person has some internal assumptions of
which he or she most likely is aware, about the reasons
why and what he or she is at this point in time. And I
also know that the Other assumes that being a knowledgeable expert I should also know why he or she is
what and where he/she is. Every Other asks this question at one point of the therapy, either after a few sessions or most often at the first session, in an implied
manner or directly. We all were taught to believe that
there is an objective reality or one objective "true" reality.
    Every person has an implicit theory of personality,
say Rosenberg and Jones (1972). A person employs categories and beliefs, of which he or she is not aware or
which are not formalized (= implicit, i.e., they have not
been put into words)—to perceive and describe characteristics of him or herself and others. There are presumably as many such theories (as well as realities, to refresh
your memory) as there are individuals. Implicit theories
have also been dubbed "common sense," "lay," and
"naive" to distinguish them from scientific theories of
personality.
    The Other is encouraged by the therapist to look
into and experience his or her own theory of living, or
implicit theory of personality.

From a different yet related angle, Tomkins (1979) talks about individuals' constructions of life according to particular scripts for interpreting, creating, enhancing, or defending a family of related scenes or happenings. In Tomkins' view, the person is like a playwright constructing a dramatic narrative to try to make sense of life (McAdams, 1988). Psychological magnification begins, says Tomkins (1979),

> in earliest infancy when the infant imagines, via co-assembly, a possible improvement in what is already a rewarding scene, attempts to do what may be necessary to bring it about, and so produces and connects a set of scenes which continue to reward him with food, and its excitement and enjoyment, and also with the excitement and enjoyment of remaking the world closer to the heart's desire. He is doing what he will continue to do all his life–to command the scenes he wishes to play. Like Charlie Chaplin, he will try to write, direct, produce, criticize, and promote the scenes in which he casts himself as hero. (pp. 214–215)

In the psychobiographic approach the Other is the narrator of his or her own implicit personality theory and has been given, and is entitled to, the role of hero or heroine in the casting of their personal scripts. The Other is the knower, the one who actually knows and holds unto the data.

I can imagine that at this point your level of excitement, if you are a psychotherapist, is at the abyss level. Are you feeling distressed because I am, you allege, taking from you any meaningful function or perceived self-affirmative script, emptying and depriving you of your professional cast as rescuer? Well, think about how the Other feels, sitting in front of your pundit's eyes or lying on the couch with your eyes behind them while the Other gazes at your impressive and intimidating office decor! Many scholarly theoretical explanations have tried to justify this self-entitled role of heroism or nobility, from social empirical findings under the heading of "placebo effect" to relatively complex and articulate psychopathological models such as Kohut's (1979) narcissistic mirroring and need for introjection of idealized self-objects in the beginning phases of psychotherapy. The "effectists jump to conclusions by using a statistical camera; but taking an exact picture of a society at unease is like trying to manufacture a strong leader in response to a survey that shows what the majority of people are craving, while in fact there is an urgent need for an in-depth analysis of a disturbing symptom."

Psychotherapy prefers to address the symptom, especially in an era of managed care and search of shortcuts in life (i.e., short-term, brief psychotherapy): let us give the people what they need—a Tylenol, a "hero." The other explanation is just a grave misunderstanding arising out of the grave juxtaposition of psychotherapeutic theory with psychopathological theory and the personification of a theoretical descriptive concept. Let me state that we, certainly I, crave an ideal father or mother. We may differ, as Freud implied, in the extent and intensity of our craving or need, yet through the years that I have worked with people who "match" (through the eyes of the DSM authors or Kohut) this category, I found with no exception that the ideal that these people, like others, craved was a humane encounter.

Then your hunch is definitely correct: you are being gradually deprived of your sources of power used for control, and not for liberation. The psychobiographic approach assumes that there is a direct link between diminishment of the power structure of psychotherapy and the psychotherapist, and the diminishment of helplessness and powerlessness of the Other. Working through this structure or theme, by the person therapist by him or herself, and together and with the help of the Other, is at the center of the psychobiographic discourse, in the beginning phases and all along.

Other: *Well, I guess I am asking you.*

I bypass the ambivalence embodied in the phrase *I guess.* Usually ambivalence is considered to be resistance to therapy or to change. Miller (Miller & Rollnick, 1991), who works with people with addictive behaviors, says: "Ambivalence is a normal and common component of many psychological problems" (p. 46). For him and for many others, ambivalence is an impediment in the way of growth, and they differ from one another in strategies they propose by which to deal with this problem. From the standpoint of psychobiographic psychotherapy, ambivalence is viewed as (1) a normal phenomenon in life, and (2) a desired component in living. And what I propose here is that ambivalence, in the therapeutic setting as well as in other life settings, is a healthy reaction, a life-preserving resistance, to a power component allegedly or actually present, and that as such it serves as a security operation. Even if we consider only the current cultural stigmatization of those who resort to psychotherapy, and the financial encumbrance it entails, it would be unnatural to expect anything other than ambivalence.

But people bring with them some emotions (i.e., biographical feelings) aside from matters of culture and finances, and these emotions outrageously claim that not they, the victims, but the perpetrators should be behind the bars of these visible or invisible mental institutions. Listen to the rage behind and beneath ambivalent feelings; that sense of contempt toward *me*, who is undetermined (i.e., helpless) and toward the historical Other, who made *me* helpless and undetermined.

The historical or environmental Other—partly because of personality makeup and partly because of cultural mores and socioeconomic practices that promulgate and enable the exploitation of the minor, the minority, and the weak—has not had the courage to live with ambivalence, as a human condition, but acted out on it, as *action* dissociated from *being* is a socioeconomically sanctioned condition. I, the person therapist, the personification of the historical and the socioeconomical, am naturally at the focus of these ambivalent feelings (the Other, the "patient," resorts less to splitting maneuvers than we would like to believe). This ambivalence is tightly intertwined with the issue of trust, another "good" one cannot purchase at the supermarket even if it is APA-accredited. Trust is to be created and to be earned by both the therapist and the Other.

Miller (Miller & Rollnick, 1991), who is a representative of other psychological strategists, says that "this working through of ambivalence is a central goal of motivational interviewing" (p. 46). Of course, he means working through the client's ambivalence, and he proceeds to offer skills other than the confrontation–denial trap to help clients break through ambivalence. What happened to the therapist's ambivalence? The strategists say that a professional must have worked through these issues in personal therapy, through countertransference analysis, or through professional readings, multiple-choice exams, practicums and internships, and so on. Here we witness how psychotherapy comes forth as a mythology of human existence. Ambivalence, I came to learn, is a human condition. Fighting my tendency as a man to use women as objects, I find myself claiming a victory, only to reveal that I am being confronted with a new problem in the battleground of ambivalence.

The Other's ambivalence, then, is respected. In other words, his or her feelings of mistrust, are trusted.

Me: *I don't know, frankly speaking. I mean it.*

If it has been said with genuine intention and conviction, it always results in astonishment and puzzlement. It is a simple and truthful sentence; yet so many "experts" find it irrelevant (Brown, 1995). I am conveying to the Other, whether he or she has paranoidlike feelings of transparency or is just an anxiety-driven neurotic, that they are the source of biological knowledge, master of this knowledge and the source of power. The Other is the playwright.

Me: *Are you surprised?*
Other: *I certainly am.*
Me: *Are you, then, pondering what you are going to get in exchange for your money?*
Other: [Expect a diverse range of affective display from mild, shy embarrassment to vexation.] *I certainly am.*
Me: *I will place all my resources, knowledge, skill, and experience at your disposal, but I have not yet met somebody like you. I have read many books on personality but either they were theoretical or they discussed somebody other than you—so that I have no idea who you are unless you tell me. I read the charts*

[when these are available] *but they are second-and third-hand impressions and they are very incomplete. You are the original and I am interested in you and in your story when you are ready to tell it.*

Pay attention to how gradually a "contract" concerning the use and division of power is being formed. Actually we are witnessing the formation of a relationship rather than a contract, in which all are assumed to have a personality which is waiting to be told or written. *Me* demonstrates active interest in the person of the Other, yet respects the person's need for autonomy as well as privacy. The Other is encouraged to tell when he or she is ready. The emphasis is on process and then on content; and the language is not contaminated with labeling and pathographizing phrases. I have used this language with all regardless of their DSM diagnosis and found it comprehensible even in the most extreme conditions. Also note the engendering of the nucleus of narration, of psychobiography. I remind the reader that it is not a strategy, a technique, or this or that kind of maneuver, but the truth. We don't have any X ray exposing the soul, mind, or personhood. We just have some scattered beams that at best light some tiny parts of the person still in need of validation. These scattered beams comprise our personal resources of what can be subsumed under Carl Rogers' heritage (1957), and extensive, actively acquired knowledge via critical thinking, and personal biography: intellectual, emotional, and professional-experiential.

Other: *Where do you want me to start?*

This utterance illustrates how traditional psychotherapy generally starts. I assume that the reader is familiar with the starting of a therapy session at the beginning phase, which can be found in any textbook on psychotherapy. Usually, after a few minutes of personal introduction—that by itself can be used to promote power-related vectors, but I will not expand on that because of diminished interest in formalities—the patient is asked something that can be subsumed under, "Tell me what brings you here?" and "What are your expectations of therapy?" Then, in accord with the psychotherapeutic school's dispositions and orientations, there follows a discussion and formulation of the problems that the patient is encountering and then, or before that, an explication of how therapy works.

Let us examine how the process of unlearning works, this time for the therapist.

CHAPTER FIFTEEN

Person Study: Rina

The person I will be describing in this vignette was not a "patient" but rather a friend of a friend who at age 38 had resorted to therapy after experiencing some difficulties with herself and in her marital life. She had attended one session of therapy, and because she seemed to my friend even more distressed than before, he suggested that she talk to me. I asked her: "What has happened that you are so bothered?" "Thank God," she said with a sigh of relief, "you are not asking what bothers *me.*"

Indeed, these two utterances, which seem naive on the surface, and between which difference may seem minute and not very important, actually represent two wholly distinct world views. One implies that you are part of the life process; the other, that you are the life process itself. One says that you are being created by history, by events, as well as creating them. The other says that you *are* the history, you are creating it. One says that the event that traumatized (i.e., bothered) you happened to you. The other says that you are the source of the event: you traumatized yourself. In other words, one says that what is outside is outside, while the other says that what is outside is inside. By now, if you still remember my first chapters, you know what had happened to this woman, but let us listen to her story:

"I cannot tell what exactly happened. Everything seemed in shape. Everything seemed to go well, but I came out of the

*session even more tense, and I cannot understand why, why
this tension, and I don't know what to do next. I want to go
back to her; she seemed okay, she understood my problems;
but it is as if my body resists me."*

It seems a naive passage, nothing extraordinary except the woman's extraordinary sensitivity to her own
body language (i.e., to her cumulative experience of the
senses). And it is correct; as I propose, it happens again
and again; it perpetuates itself. What? you are asking.

In response to my inquiry, she said that her problems were dealt with, formulated, and processed to her
full satisfaction, and she presented a list of the problems
she and her therapist had decided she needed to work
on. When we seemed at an impasse, I asked her gently,
"Rina, can you please tell me, what are your concerns
in life?" Verbatim, this is what she said:

*"Concerns! Oh, well, now I am concerned . . .
funny . . . what I am gonna bring to her the next session . . .
is that what you mean . . . because . . . well . . . you know
. . . what am I going to do with my MSW . . . I got it rather
late in life . . . though my husband says it is like an old
wine. . . . "* ("It seems to me that you don't know exactly
what to do with your new sense of your new freedom,
am I right?" You should have seen her face: a newborn
bird pumping its wings.) *"Damn right . . . though frightening, but I am proud . . . I think we both [she and her
husband] don't know what to do with it . . . "* ("Did you
talk about this with her [the therapist]?") *"Oh no, this
is not a problem, is it! Wait a minute. . . . "*

She is right: she doesn't have problems, she has concerns. Yet she was being treated, in a professional and
sophisticated manner, as a problem. She was objectified
in a learned manner, yet she did not deny her experience, which ultimately rescued her from a long, expensive—emotionally as well as financially—and dubious

"therapeutic" journey. The technologist looks for problems, as the mechanic looks for "what is wrong (the problem) with this machine" to be fixed, whereas people have concerns.

Me: *You may want to share with me some of your concerns?*

The notion of "concern" carries some transforming qualities by depathographizing and thus humanizing the I–thou interaction. When Rina said she was concerned about what to bring for discussion the next session, she was actually reflecting on her sense of loneliness. Many supervisees are also familiar with this very source of alienation. They, as well as their counterpart in therapy sessions, are expected to take responsibility and bring substance. In many instances it resembles the businesslike exchange of goods, except that the material in this case is emotional problems. I asked Rina what concerned her about the upcoming session. She said she was afraid she would find herself engaging in a grueling game whereby one takes the role of a producing machine and the other of quality controller. "She [the therapist] was so focused on my problems," Rina mumbled. I asked Rina why she didn't voice her concerns. "What should I have told her? That I don't want her to focus on my problems? Isn't that why I reached out for her? she would say, and I would have to agree with her [i.e., incriminate myself] while I am not actually sure." Besides, Rina felt her therapist might have thought she was too suspicious of her (i.e., she is paranoid). She feared being "so lonely there, me and my problems" in front of an anonymous person, a depersonalized voice machine, analyzing "her."

Many supervisees are familiar with this process when session after session they have to bring material to fill up, unempty, the otherwise rather blank hour because of lack of the personal (and) dialogue. This whole atmosphere disempowers the Other—"I feel belittled," Rina said—but empowers the dissociative processes by intensifying the dissociation of the praxis of therapy from the experience of that same therapy. Rina, serving as a prototype, was distressed because of a *disparity of expectations* (see Introduction) according to which she entered a setting, called therapy, with an implicit craving that she would be treated and understood as a whole and as a person, that she would be looked at through her own time agency (i.e., through a personal life context); yet she confronted a reality which denied her herself and treated her as an object. She entered therapy in order to defeat her paralysis, but she found out only that it had been exacerbated. She left the session more defeated; that is what she felt, though according to formal criteria, the session went well.

Rina resumed "therapy," with the hope that this time her protest would be heard and thus she would be relieved of her distress—her paralysis, a dissociation between intention-motivation and action. The expert-oriented therapy intensified her dissociative processes because it addressed her problems (i.e., behavioral, dynamic-interpersonal, etc.) but not her experience. It insisted on seeing her as a problem awaiting repair, in contrast to seeing her as a person amidst a crisis in life. Concern is an experiential, nonpathographizing concept which integrates emotions (biographical feelings), perceptions (cognitions, beliefs, etc.), and experience (the above + bodily sensations). That experience encompasses both knowledge and affects was acknowledged by Tomkins (1979) when he said: "A world experienced without any affect would be a pallid, meaningless world. We would know *that* things happened, but we could not care whether they did or not" (p. 203).

A psychobiographic approach to a meeting between me and the Other strives for an interpersonal *experience* which has never occurred before, in the sense that it has occurred only in the earliest power-absent phase of human development. From the earliest phase, *me* strives to eliminate and convert the sense of coercion, defeat, and punishment, into a sense of autonomy, choice, growth, exploration, and discovery of each through each. There are many creative routes to achieve this goal; the psychobiographic approach serves as one. In such an approach, in which, to reremind the reader, the emphasis is on a philosophy of psychotherapy, on a philosophy of relationship, more than a technique, *me* is attentive to:

What is the nature of the Other's protest?
What is the Other concerned about?

CHAPTER SIXTEEN

Person Study: Lois

Lois exemplifies some of the working assumptions of the psychobiographic approach. I met her when she was 19 and had a history of major depression with psychotic features dating back 2 years. She had had five psychiatric admissions following her parents' separation, and multiple suicide attempts as well as episodes of self-mutilation. She felt unloved by others, hated and despised herself, and felt excessive guilt over being a "bad person." She reported auditory and visual hallucinations, and withdrew from any social life. In partial remission, she was referred to me for psychotherapy with a revised diagnosis of Major Depression Disorder, severe with psychotic features on Axis I, and schizotypal traits as well as borderline traits on Axis II. I did not agree with the revised classification, which seemed to have been offered (i.e., reinterpreted) to justify an antipsychotic medication, but accepted it because Lois's condition was very unstable and she was a young woman at very high risk. This is the short descriptive history of her sickness, and let us now turn to her person.

When reading clinical reports, I always wonder about their validity. Naturally they are inherently subjective, yet they are perceived by their authors as being definitively objective and valid. So many behaviors that seem bizarre through the preset prisms of a diagnostician's mind may reveal themselves to be rather logical

through the contextual eyes of a heurist or phenomenologist. The classic example is that of Kraepelin, cited
and analyzed ingeniously by Laing (1965). For that reason, when the Other is said to have "poor, or no, eye
contact," I do not displace my own eyes with his or hers.
Lois was looking at me from the beginning. My eyes
were responsive to her, holding onto her, yet respecting
her and unpossessive. They were not threatening, but
just there for her to approach them whenever she desired to. I stress this fact because Lois was not using her
mouth for communication. And she did not for almost
5 months. I did all the talking during this time, two
sessions a week, 45 minutes each. When she opened her
mouth I could not believe my ears because she uttered
with a set voice: "*It is all about power. . . .*"

The approach advocated here is one that strives to
create an interpersonal experience and atmosphere devoid of power maneuvers and serving as primary alimentary symbiosis. Here are some general guidelines for
creating such a growth-promoting experience. I should
again remind the reader that who one is, is more crucial
than what one says, the assumption being granted that
if one is, then one also has a say.

Lois' silence was interpreted for what it was—a protest. In a nonpathographizing approach such notions as
emptiness, deterioration, impoverishment, and so forth
are perceived as security operations employed by a person therapist who at a given time is in an experiential
stupor regarding the Other's personal, emotional, and
intellectual attributes. The fact that I cannot understand
you, for example, doesn't say as much about you as
about me. I am lacking; I am experiencing lack. Accordingly, one scans for the positive, for the life-giving and
empowering, for the strengths. A dear psychiatrist and

supervisor used to remind me, "If you find yourself not liking someone, look for something to like. There should be something." And Friedman (cited in Stern, 1985) encourages us to treat "the patient as though he were roughly the person he is about to become. The patient will explore being treated that way, and will fill in the personal details."

As is implied from the extended usage of the term *trauma*, the protest is always connected to objectification whether episodic or continual. Objectification means, as has been said, power used in order to depersonalize the Other, and using the Other as a means to an end which is selfish in nature. Listening to the protest implies care and respect: *nonindifference*. It necessitates empathy with the anguish and the anguished, with the pain and the sufferer. It implies responsiveness: you are important to me, I respect you, I take you seriously. In my view this is the true nature of love in psychotherapy. Here I enlarge the meaning of *real-interpersonal-interaction* in my definition of psychobiographic psychotherapy (see p. 109).

Lois' privacy was respected in every move, and by that I mean her right, her constitutional right, like that of every citizen labeled normal or labeled by the DSM, to hold onto her thoughts, feelings, and fantasies, and share them, if at all, whenever and with whomever she chose to. This message was conveyed to her, just as at this moment it is being conveyed to you, and as it is conveyed to anybody in a psychobiographic meeting. She was told that trust is to be gained, and that it is not easily gained; that there was no reason for her at this time to trust me just because I was titled a psychologist, but that I asked her to consider giving it, gradually and cautiously, a chance. I shared myself with her—pieces of my professional biography (disclosure) such as when an 18-year-old man with whom I was meeting for the 7th month approached me after a pretty long vacation with "I missed you." It was the first time he referred to me with a positive verbalized affection and I noticed how laborious it was for him. He certainly took a risk of exposing himself to vulnerability. When I told him that I missed him, too, which I really did, he started to make funny faces, laughed, and said, "My father always says I love you, so what?" How does one know when something said is real?

Remembering our discussion of therapy and therapists as enemies, it is astonishing how at times some experts treat the issue of trust in a superficial and cursory manner such as confronting the Other with, "You have a problem with trust," "You should work on your issue of trust," "She doesn't have basic trust," misusing an Eriksonian notion, and the like, oblivious of the fact that in an alienated society we all have "a problem with trust." Trust as a value is faceless in a society in which in order to survive one should learn, and actually is taught, how to manipulate rather than trust people.

During the *establishing a relationship phase* (a personal term I prefer over the schizoid–businesslike "contract"), the concept of mutuality is introduced by *Me* by stressing my part with such complementary phrases as: "I will be honest, too," "I, too, will be open," "I, too, will be on time," etc.

Second, Lois' reality was accepted. I just believed her, and believed in her subjective experience. I made it explicit that I believed that something had been inflicted upon her, and that no matter what had happened and what she had done she had good reasons for her feelings and thoughts. The Others in a psycho-biographic approach are being reassured that the focus is not on what went wrong (i.e., morbid) but what made their lives flow the way they did. What were the events, people, and circumstances that led to their lives flowing one way rather than another? Notice how the seeds of a life story and a life history approach are being planted. Also note the absence of the following components in this formulation: fantasies and cognitions. This respect for another's, including the Other's, reality is the propelling force behind many cases of recovery in therapy by counteracting the impact of negative affects such as guilt, shame, self-disgust, and so forth. When emerging out of her mutism, Lois anchored herself time and again by reminding herself: "I lied . . . I hid things . . . nobody was listening, I thought it was unbelievable . . . *There must have been some reason that I lied.*" She was actually saying that she was not born a liar; it was developmental, it was historical. She had incorporated my firm belief in her being victimized by an objectifying reality whose real nature as of that time was still obscure. When I commented on her long silence, she said, "Sometimes I want to cry; it's frustration, not sadness." There was no doubt left that her silence was a protest, was a cry: I was not being taken seriously (a common practice in a society in which people are treated as commodities).

Any relationship at times entails taking risks. I made many efforts to fight Lois' tendency to mutilate herself. In the matter of safety I know no compromise. I knew that this was the real test of my true intentions, my *non-indifference,* and that though Lois might put on a front of defiance and carelessness, she was in fact minutely observing to see if I was indeed trustworthy and serious.

I insisted that she stop seeing a boyfriend with whom she was engaging in self-mutilation and other behaviors that were potentially dangerous. "In this case," I said to her, "it is you, no one else, who is abusing yourself, and to that I cannot agree; otherwise in my eyes I am considered a participant. I know you might hate me or be angry at me for that but I also know you will appreciate it later." The parents were contacted, contracted, and instructed about the exact measures they should employ in case Lois attempted to contact her boyfriend.

This is definitely an example of misery inflicted by the person from within the person, with her particular self-mutilative behaviors comprising symbolization and specific meanings that were discussed and clarified. However, it had happened exactly because the prevailing social system demonstrated a readiness to convert a misery inflicted upon a person to misery inflicted from within a person: Neither the mother nor the father had attempted at any time to put an end to it. As we will see, they didn't now, either.

Reflecting back on some theoretical postulates of the psychobiographic approach, we notice the following: *Me* dispels the power of anonymity of the person therapist by being emotionally and intellectually reactive-interactive, and through sharing our own biography. Sharing is at the root of any therapeutic relationship, either with a mother, child, wife, friend, boss, or psychotherapist; nevertheless, contrary to any other relationships, in psychotherapy it is conceived as unilateral. Some psychotherapists, as well as their counterparts, just do not know how to share or what to share. Sharing is the antithesis of hoarding, and in a materialistic society where competition for goods is a person's pivot of action, people are taught that sharing is a commodity for exchange for some tangible relief of psychosomatic tension or material profit. Sharing exposes a person to vulnerabilities precarious to existence in a power-oriented society. In such a society people are taught to withhold, but without appearing to do so, because our culture cannot tolerate the idea that people are actually enemies to one another. Knowledge is power, and in sharing that, one exposes oneself to vulnerabilities as well as disposing of the very source of that power. However, some are concerned that sharing, making therapy personal and intimate, will expose the profession to malpractice and misconduct. That is a genuine concern which reflects on our mistrust of ourselves as human beings and on a correct judgment of ourselves as just human beings susceptible to human feebleness. And it should be so as long as knowledge, cherished by itself and apart from life and personal integrity—in the form of dry, depersonalized lectures, hoarding CE credits, or piling up research papers—is at the pivot of the current education and preparation of mental health practitioners.

In the psychobiographic approach, personal integrity underlies the firm belief in the appropriateness and inevitability of mutual sharing—of emotions (biographical feelings) and of experiences (biographical happenings, whether professional or otherwise).

Paradoxically, from the moment the Other steps into my room, an invisible presupposition is being made between us regarding a general hierarchic situation. Though formal and impersonal, it, nevertheless, reflects upon the Other's basic trust of Me's integrity and proficiency. Psychotherapy is ever, as long as it lasts, and in every moment of its duration, a nonstop process of negotiation of power in interpersonal relationships. If the negotiation is successful and each feels he or she has been given a fair share, then therapy continues until a different power vector is sought and negotiated. However, there is along the continuum a turning point in which the impersonal becomes personal and the Other agrees and decides to take the risk of giving the Me a position of power. Me is perceived as being sincere, with integrity and wisdom. This is one of those special moments of psychotherapy, as well as of any other interpersonal meeting, in which a personal choice regarding another person is being made, and I will expand on this later.

Self-disclosure should always reflect on Me's integrity, personal or impersonal, and the hierarchic position. As such, disclosures of sexual–erotic fantasies and sexual biography violate the integrity and the agreed hierarchic position of the parties. As in any real (i.e., nontechnical) relationship, biographical self-disclosure demands: (1) modulation of quantity: it should be given in a dosage appropriate to the Other, and (2) modulation of timing: it should be given at a time appropriate to the Other. However, I recommend two more safeguards to protect self-disclosure from being an exercise in manipulation, self-centered self-aggrandizement, or self-centered tension release. Self-disclosure in the psychobiographic approach aims at discerning what is common to us as human beings, such as fears, shames, anxieties, hates, angers, loves and sex, successes and failures. It aims at conveying the essence of Sullivan's (1955) comment that "we are all much more simply human than otherwise," (p. 16) even though what being "simply human" means is construed in various ways. An example of such a self-disclosure would be a man's struggle not to objectify a woman, and it can be illustrated by a personal story which involves such a theme with its accompanying affects, provided it answers the content and timing prerequisites mentioned above.

The other safeguard is nothing more than what is actually known to any critical independent thinker: do not impose yourself on others nor on the data. Accordingly, I say the following after an expression of feelings (and by this I further anchor the feelings in a specific happening) or any biographical self-disclosure:

Me: *Well, this was my experience* (feeling). *Different people have different experiences* (different feelings). *What was your experience* (feeling)?

The other kind of biographical self-disclosure which is absent in a psychobiographic meeting relates to any belief system—including but not limited to political, ideological, religious, or psychological—which contains a potential for becoming indoctrination. In a psychobiographic meeting, self-disclosure is introduced as a means to humanize and mutualize a rather technical and unilateral profession, and to abolish the anonymity of the person therapist and his or her alleged technique as a source of power exertion. On the positive side, as already mentioned, self-disclosure provides a demarcated humane psychobiographer who is clear and known to the Other. Such self-disclosures are tolerated within a psychobiographic approach as long as they illuminate human variance and difference and thus do not violate the prerequisites for a pluralistic approach in understanding a human being's life. I did not leave Jon, a minister and a former client of mine, to live long in obscurity about my being a nonreligious Jew. With him facing death due to multiple medical conditions including severe heart disease, we were able to build upon the two different faiths' view of life and death to enrich ourselves. I will always remember the sessions in which we struggled through our fears and apprehensions, finding out that we were both human beings, and in solidarity. We shared many biographical stories concerning our religious upbringings and gradually Jon could find a new meaning in those stories about himself, about his parents' religious and other practices, and about what made his life flow the way it did. When separating, he said, "You will remain alive in me," and I knew his soul saluted life. I salute you, Jon. Thank you.

As a freshman I was tormented with guilt that "they give me more than I give them." "Maybe you take more," said Gila, whom I was lucky to have as my first supervisor. Since then I know that as long as that kind of guilt feelings is with me I am still breathing the true spirit of psychology.

The hours with Lois were filled with what I thought were relevant biographical stories. I let myself be creative, giving myself the freedom to make mistakes, to be real-human, and not real-professional, as I thought that a well-equipped Me, or person therapist, should be able to move back and forth between both. At times I talked about her apparent diagnostic symptoms, about medication, and about "losing our heads," yet immediately I relaxed her anxieties: *any* of us can go crazy. Now and then I would stop and ask her: *"Lois, I cannot go on. I need your feedback. Does what I say make any sense to you?"*

She would nod her head signaling "Yes." When she did not like something, or when I felt she was angry at me or at something related to me and got up to leave the office, I would reassure her of my concern for her and that I would be there for her the next session. I want to vouch for the Other that though we are equals, some privileges are reserved exclusively for him or her, Me being essentially unshakeable, steady, concerned, and earnest.

Lois got to know the story about the willpower of a mother bird who one spring tried diligently to provide a warm shelter for her babies by building her nest in the middle of the vent duct of my dryer, causing a dangerous gas leak and a hot familial debate about the course of action to be taken. I told Lois how I felt when I was assigned as the "executive" in charge of cleaning up the duct, a wearisome job lasting almost a whole hour, and about my emotionally loaded dialogue with the unseen bird whose devotion, industry, and pertinacity I praised, admired, and envied, even while I hated her and was angry at her for causing me so much trouble, and forcing me to deprive her of shelter for herself and her babies. And Lois would listen to my thoughts about personality; about what some others say and I dislike, and what is attractive to me and why; and about how I managed to turn around my inferiority feelings, as Alfred Adler would say, during adolescence. In my understanding of personality development, I said to her, nobody is born bad; being evil is a self-determination to be so by a series of decisions and choices regarding power. Usually these evil-minded people do not populate psychotherapeutic clinics. They flourish outside the clinics.

Next to psychobiographical and personality data, in a psychobiographic meeting I rely extensively on developmental psychology, and much more often on developmental tasks confronting a person than on developmental lapses a person has been afflicted with. While psychotherapy is in motion, I fight any temptation to resort to psychopathologizing and labeling, finding that I do so whenever I am in a state of "more": more anxious, more angry, more uncertain than the Other. Then I make genuine effort to recapture the last session, or the moment of "more" that just elapsed and irritated me to a point where I desperately needed the DSM—it is indeed an act of desperation on these particular occasions—to discern what went wrong. More often than not, I find out that this moment occurs whenever there is an interpersonal disjunction between Me and the Other. And, as I contend, this disjunction occurs as a response to an objectifying process and/or incident utilized by Me, denying the wholeness of and further alienating the Other.

How do I know, you may be wondering, that I was doing the right things with Lois? What guided me at a particular moment of choice to pick between so many categories of affectional and epistemological content? Was I actually doing what I so vehemently have protested against?

There was no session, or portion of a session, in which the Other, Lois or someone else, was not fully active in defining and directing the nature of the meeting. As said, at each and every meeting Me offers a *demarcated primal relationship,* its nature spelled out earlier in this section, that above all provides the Other with a nonoppressive and safe *interpersonal experience* from which to explore the relationship to him or herself, and to others including Me, and the person's future relationships. It was Lois who instructed me to supply that affectional and psychological food she desperately needed and could not verbalize with words. She gave me feedback whenever I asked, or volunteered feedback, by her eyes, subtle facial expressions, and body postures. Of course, in choosing the content of my stories I relied heavily on my intuition, and on hospitalization charts and interviews with her parents. Correctly perceived, I was engaged in interpretations but in the same vein as life and living are interpretations. Notice that the experience itself, I of her and she of me, and not any theoretical postulate determined and dictated the spontaneous selection of the specific categories of biographical/developmental disclosure. Lois was raped physically and psychologically. It was all about power. She "interpreted" Me, caressing her wounds with words. With Lois, as well as with others, I was following the psychobiographic spirit that the person is the knower and the interpreter.

With this in mind let us turn to the next person study in order to illustrate some other propositions for a psychobiographic approach.

CHAPTER SEVENTEEN

Person Studies: Me/Other, Fritz

In Part 1, chapters 2 and 3, I discussed the adverse effects of displacement of a primary source with a secondary one on the division of power in the psychotherapeutic dyad, and eventually on the person-to-person relationship and the therapeutic outcome.

She: *There is no therapy without a bond, a relation.*

He: *A relation that enables and facilitates growth. . . .*

She: [silence]

He: *Who put me in the position to tell others who or what they are or what they feel?*

She: *If they were not looking for somebody to tell them what to do they wouldn't have come to therapy!*

He: *He who has a stand takes a stand; he who has a value system, who is capable of value judgment, is not neutral, is critical, does* not *accept anything without using an internal self-filter. An intellectual, a thinker, by nature is not an accepting person. Acceptance, by definition, is a matter of process. Acceptance of something unknown or unfamiliar is not acceptance, but takeover.*

She: *It's too abstract, we are working with people.*

He: *Philosophy?*

She: *We are psychologists.*

He: *Psychology was philosophy before being turned into physiology.*

She: *Are you playing smart?*

He: *I am thinking, of a trap, if one thinks, one is abstract; if one doesn't, one lacks ego strength, id driven.*

She: *Let's get back to work.*

He: *Are you saying it's my personality?*

She: [silence]

He: *Thinking is working, too.*

She: *Well . . .*

He: *Why do you think you feel and understand my client better than I?*

She: *I may say I have some experience with such kinds of patients.*

He: *Have you treated his twin?*

She: *Are you playing smart again?*

He: *What are such kinds of patients?*

She: *Don't play around; you know.*

He: *Such as California apples and Vermont apples?*

She: *Oof, he is a character disorder!*

He: *He said he is Mark.*

She: *He is a killer!*

He: *He says he is a patriot; he was serving his country.*

She: *He must have some feelings about that, did you ask him?*

He: *I did; he said he is not connected with it.*

She: *He is repressing it from memory.*

He: *How do you know?*

She: [silence]

He: ***He** doesn't have anything to do with it; dissociation saved his life by enabling him to take a life.*

She: *He is not conscious of it.*

He: *Are you suggesting I make the unconscious conscious?*

She: *Otherwise he would kill again.*

He: *Or because of that. . . .*

She: *He might get some control over his impulses.*

He: *He knows he is aggressive.*

She: *You make me feel helpless.*

He: *I do not.*

She: *As he makes you feel helpless, maybe. . . .*

He: *He doesn't make me feel helpless; I do not feel helpless with him.*

She: *You are offended at being supervised. . . .*

This was an imaginary yet real dialogue between Other, who in a different setting is Me, and Me, who became Other just after the above meeting. It is imaginary because She was not aware of this dialogue that I conducted with her in my notebook at one of the supervision sessions. I wonder how many "patients" follow the same praxis of saying something and writing down something else in the privacy of their soul. Gaps and again gaps. Let us see how we can close the gap.

The above passage exemplifies how two persons with actually terribly distinct world views are being engaged in a clash seemingly with regard to practical issues concerning the treatment (well-being) of Mark. In the first section of this work I dealt with the situation where two people, called therapist and supervisor, are using the same data, the so-called patient, though one is in a direct, personal contact and the other is in an impersonal, indirect contact. At present I am focusing on the direct contact between these two persons discussing an issue: how Mark (i.e., a problem, a concern) should be approached. One world view says it knows what the question/problem is, and how it should be resolved. In other words, *She* says: "I know what his psychological disease is, he has a character problem; he cannot modulate aggression because of some repressed memories that apparently originate from some yet unknown oedipal constellation. This is the problem; these are the goals; he made a connection with you; let's get to work."

The other world view says it is not sure. We should think, generate hypotheses, and then approach the field and look for validation. He says, I do not know what the problem is; I may have some conjectures, as the Other himself may, but the reason that impels one to begin therapy may not be the same as the one that keeps the person continuing to come to therapy; we can talk about that together and set the goals for therapy. Everything is interpretation; consequently, the Other's interpretation is as valid as mine or yours.

The meeting ended with another pathographizing caveat: "You cannot accept supervision." Actually, the meeting terminated supervision. For a few weeks afterwards I made desperate efforts to establish a working-together atmosphere despite our differences (I and her as of Me and Other) in personality and predominantly differences in politics, modes, and morals (London, 1964) of psychotherapy. These efforts failed, from my point of view, and I stopped going to her. Why? What are the theoretical and practical implications of this Me and Other encounter for the science of psychotherapy?

The wisdom of common sense insinuates that imposing one's view on another means simply dictatorship. The mental health field is of huge dimensions yet vague boundaries, comprised of more than 800 kinds of therapy and overlapping many other disciplines, from the exact science of physics to the purely spiritual. Many mental health practitioners are lost within this field, and resort to some sort of autocratic and dogmatic method of psychological understanding which is actually a world view, an interpretation, a specific kind of reality, under the guise of science. Each choice represents a personal deprivation, or, if you prefer, a personal theory of personality, life, and living. At any rate, it is a personal subjective choice; not an objective scientific one. The "patient," on the other hand, is being warded off, deprived of this same choice, the very reason why he or she came to therapy, like the very reason why Me went for psychotherapy, personally, or as a career, or both, and is being compelled to accept Me's takeover. From a world-encompassing ocean enriched and revived by the fresh and constant flow of immense rivers and melting icebergs, crossed by black and white, yellow and red creatures, the practice of psychotherapy has come to be like a small pond in New Hampshire thirsty for the seasonal penurious falls and occasional passing by of visitors. Psychotherapy tragically has cut itself off from experience. The experience of plurality, and of the interdisciplinary, endows psychotherapy with depth; and although I may admit that initially it confers also some confusion, I should immediately add that creativity succeeds confusion, just as it was said at the beginning, "There was formless and void—chaos."

I did not oppose supervision. I opposed her supervision. I opposed her oppressing my world view and imposing on me her own, coercing me to disown my very experience. I resisted an actual power component present in the meeting, in the person of the therapist, who resisted checking for her *real* self hiding behind an *expert* self. To prevent misunderstandings, I could have written the same dialogue with anybody who adheres to an all-encompassing monistic world view. Incidentally, she was psychoanalytically oriented.

As said before, autonomy is developmental, and it occurs within the context of human relatedness. How can we maximize the sense of autonomy, and consequently maximize positive affects, as we did with the depathographizing process, by minimizing the danger when at a certain point Me becomes to believe that Me knows how Other should feel, think, and behave, and how Other should be redeemed, as Me understands the concept of redemption for Other?

Here are some propositions for the person therapist:

- *Does it (the happening) have anything to do with me or with our relationship?*

Many premature terminations of psychotherapy, as well as many incidents in psychotherapy, are connected to the nature of the relationship, of the relatedness. Though some termination and incidents may originate in transferential reactions, so to speak, many others reflect a real (i.e., nonimaginative, nontransferential) and actual mishap between the person Me and the person Other, a mishap related to exertion of some sort of power.

Fritz

Fritz, a 32-year-old single black male, was referred to me for supportive psychotherapy with a diagnosis of personality disorder, schizoid, passive–aggressive, and obsessive traits. The main object, it was stated by the referring

psychiatrist, would be to prepare him for vocational rehabilitation since his parents, who were supporting him,
were getting too old and would be unable at some point
to provide for him further. But it seemed that Fritz himself was much less sure about his goals in life as well as
in therapy. In an interview with another staff member,
he mentioned a few times a disturbing habit of talking
to himself constantly since early childhood. "I cannot
control it," he complained.

Though I acknowledged the importance of vocational rehabilitation in his specific case, nevertheless, as
a rule [on its rationale I have labored so far] I refrain
from one-sided therapist-imposed goals for people who
are neither feeble-minded (otherwise, generally speaking they wouldn't have been in therapy) nor business-
minded (for the same reasons). Hence, I ventured, if I
could find the appropriate timing, to talk it over with
Fritz. And here a surprise awaited me. He refused. I
assumed he had his own reasons and eventually I proved
to be right in believing him. So I dropped the issue. But
we encountered another issue. I say "we," because as
you and I are "we," so were he and I. The sessions ran
exactly this way: the first third he would give a brief
noncommittal response to my questions with a very un-
usual rhythmic voice pattern. At one point, approximately during the second third, he would talk to himself
aloud about any formal subject that came to his mind;
then he would stop suddenly, withdraw into himself,
and start to read an always handy newspaper he brought
in. Obviously, the sessions were futile and, I thought,
there was no meeting: he was just enacting his old habit
of talking to himself. I was wrong. As has been implied,
there is no bad session, generally speaking; there is a
"bad" meeting.

Two months passed. My trials-and-errors seemed to turn out relentlessly as errors. I was helpless, and more than that, frustrated and tired of being manipulated, controlled, objectified. I looked in vain again and again into my practice with him trying to identify some unresolved issues or some resistance on my side to refrain from mysterious power exertions. At one of those recurring moments when I felt my eyelids were cast of iron, I referred to Fritz:

Me: *I honestly wonder why you are coming to me; it seems you are not interested in talking to me and in my feedback—does it have anything to do with me?*

He: [He sneers, his huge black eyes bolder than ever, staring at me as if he were watching an animal in the zoo.] *You remind me of a raccoon.*

I was stunned, as you may imagine. And as usual, my attempts to make sense of him were amounting to zero. I went home. I looked in the mirror at my eyes and I saw what he had seen. I got what was happening. Next session, after the initial greetings, I opened:

Me: *I see you have much interest in what happens in the world; do you buy a newspaper every day?*

He: *Yes, I believe people should look beyond their immediate surroundings. I like reading books, too.* [He shows me a book hidden beneath the newspaper, on some environmental topic.]

Me: *Anything interesting there?* [We look together at the newspaper.]

Me: *Nothing interesting in particular?*

He: *There are some new movies.*

Me: *Do you like movies?*

He: *Sometimes, if it is an interesting subject. Today most movies are about sex and violence.*

Me: *Is it an interesting subject for you?*

He: *No, I am not into it, are you?*

Me: *Well, I like sex, but as far as violence goes, sometimes just for entertainment, if it is not too violent; I have liked Hercules since I was a child.*

He: *You do have children, don't you? Do you hit them, you know, for educational reasons?*

Me: *No, never; should I?*

He: *My father says it is okay if it is for discipline, and I believe him.*

Me: *There are other means to discipline.*

He: *Such as persuasion by talking or a firm attitude?*

Me: *Exactly.* [He stares at me, the same eyes but not sneering.] *Did he hit you?*

For the next 35 minutes Fritz described how as a child his father used to beat him up, at times with a baseball bat, how he forced him not to cry and if he did he was beaten up again until he stopped. Mother did not spare her share and occasionally beat him on his head. He was expected to be compliant, perfect, pleasing, "a robot." He was raised in "a household like in Austria or Germany." The same fate awaited him at school. He was diagnosed as having a specific learning disability and attended a special school where he was the prey of the older children. I do not want to expand on the sequel of the treatment of this fascinating person, but psychological evaluation revealed that despite powerful emotional developmental experiences, and severe specific neurological impairment, he had been able to retain some high-functioning intellectual capabilities. He talked to himself to avoid emotional death.

What did I see in the mirror? That there was an invitation for meeting but I was blind. *I* did not meet him. I was like a psychological raccoon watching for its prey, a beaten quarry, humiliated and degraded. I was sitting there as a knowledgeable authority, like his father, using words, like his father, in the name of his psychoeducational benefit, as his father had done, and what next, naturally, one would wonder? I heard him protesting: All my life, at home, at school, I was being treated as an inferior, unequal, no good, and that is exactly what you are doing to me, chasing after my defects, my emotional handicaps; you are beating me too, with words, you are smart, you show off. In short, unwittingly, I was defeating Fritz, perpetuating his predicament. Next session I met him where *he* was, and where *he* needed me. I followed my teacher's advice: "Just one small step ahead, Herzel, no more," Dr. Marberg used to say. I did not like my image in the mirror. So when I met him next I had a different countenance and a different expression in my eyes and I greeted him as I would a neighbor with a daily newspaper poked under his arm.

When I did not play expertism by imposing self-serving goals, Fritz, the Other, had the freedom to explore his own goals, only if he could be trusted and given the chance to do so. By usurping this act from a person we actually declare them to be not a free person but a slave, an alien. By this practice, by usurping a person's basic right to set their own goals and negotiate for them on an equal basis, we are actually treating that person as a lunatic, chaining them to invisible walls, pretending to be not doing so. And there is no revolution on the horizon.

Fritz did not want to fear me, as he "feared him," his father; and he did not "respect him" either, but he did want to respect me if only I, unlike his father who "never nurtured" him, could care enough to take his "feelings seriously." I did so when I sincerely asked him what he didn't like about me! You, he heard me saying, have meaning to me; you are not an object.

The following quote is a synopsis of the power structure of psychotherapy and its relation to pathographizing processes ("mistakes"). The speaker is Fritz at our separation meeting.

> If you were a teacher of psychology and you would complain hard about their [my students'] mistakes instead of harping on their accomplishments—you must have had supervisors like that—you become resistant and go over your mistakes. I don't mind having power over them [others] but a lot of people don't know how to use authority . . . I have to be careful what I say because my father supports me, but when I get independent . . . you did not try to manipulate or exploit me. . . .

I–thou entails understanding. Understanding entails interpretation, of whatever sort. A psychobiographer, one who knows one's biography and psychology, in interactions with the Other, may need interpretations either for understanding the interpersonal and the Other, or for helping the Other to understand him or herself—to know his or her own biography and psychology. Whether psychoanalytic, cognitive, biographic, or otherwise, an interpretation, in the hands of a certified doctrinaire, has the potential of becoming a tool for control, manipulation, and indoctrination, as I have demonstrated throughout this work. These two propositions advance the idea that the Other is the source of his or her own knowledge (current and previous biography) and therefore it is the Other who is the validator. The Other is being released of any subordination to any theory, monistic or pluralistic, or therapist.

I habitually remind the Other that I actually do not know him or her; I do not know how and what that person feels, thinks, or wants, that there is no book in the entire universe about them; that I won't know unless they tell me, whenever they want to, and whatever they want to, provided they are honest and open, as much as they can afford at that moment, and as much as they feel me to be open and honest. And I repeat over and over before I am going to launch an affective or ideational interpretation, "Please do not forget to correct me if I am wrong." By this practice I also attain another objective of the psychobiographic approach:

A life without history is akin to a plant without its soil. The Other, it was assumed, though dissociated from portions of his life history, due to massive objectifying processes, is still the Owner of it. Fritz was there. He felt then. He ideated. And he was engaged in the dissociations. I have shown how a specific power-absent experiential dimension of the meeting between the person therapist, the person Other, and the ensuing interpersonal relationship serves to dedissociate the dissociated. Another way of achieving this same objective, very familiar to every student of personality assessment, is asking the person a question. Again, the manner of asking is as important as, if not more important than, the question itself, and the requirements of quantity and timing should be applied here as well.

Biographical questions, in contrast to the more formal interview questions, are attempts to close gaps in memory, by unraveling the important aspects of the Other's experience, and their motivational, affective, and cognitive preemptives and consequences. A heuristic psychobiographer revitalizes in the Other the passion to know, the curiosity to deepen, and the motivation to reach beyond the apparent. The Other will gradually assume the role of explorer of their own *I.* The person will learn that *I* is to be created in a constant, ever-flowing process of *unlearning.* As life progresses, the same questions of life—love, god, death, and money—need to be unlearned and learned anew, to be reexperienced for the sake of remaining alive, still loving, and breathing the spirit of life.

A psychobiographic person therapist asks him or herself as well as the Other: *How much power do I really need, and what for?* Being "the universal solvent of human relations" (Siu, 1979, p. 40), power is ever present in the meeting, any meeting, and should be initiated by Me for discussion by way of questions such as: *Am I coercing myself on you? Do you feel belittled somehow by me or by something I said, or some kind of feeling like that? If at any point you feel I am imposing anything, just let me know; we can talk about that.* This way, the Other becomes aware of interpersonal cues related to power exertion and objectification for control, an awareness that has been hampered, as Fritz said, by constant exposure to manipulations by oppressive people and situations. Me and Other are actually experiencing the dispowering of helplessness—yet another instance of "corrective emotional experience."

Two other propositions that are important in the therapeutic relationship are:

- *Correct me if I am wrong.*
- *Wastebasket.*

The prompt "Correct me if I am wrong" serves three functions: (1) The Other is the site of authority, the Knower, and thus, is empowered; (2) It serves as a requirement for the Other to constantly activate an internal filter to test external and the more critical internal stimuli. You may liken this function to that of the observing ego. (3) In the psychobiographic approach the Other is the researcher and the ultimate source of judgment and validation. The prompt serves Me to validate the Other's interventions. "Validity," Lee Cronbach reminds us, "is subjective rather than objective: the plausibility of the conclusion is what counts. And plausibility, to twist a cliché, lies in the ear of the beholder" (cited in Bruner, 1990, p. 108).

I use the wastebasket example with people who are extremely insecure in interpersonal exchange and haunted by severe fears of being overwhelmed, intruded upon, and overcome by another's knowledgeability. Roughly, I say something like: *"We are here to give each other feedback. I might have some ideas about what you say that I want to share with you; it might be totally off track; in that case don't hesitate to use the wastebasket."* Many instead use me, which was the original intention, and in many instances it becomes a joke to have fun with. I have used it with colleagues to melt down the same barriers and enable us to engage in true unlearnings.

Let us now turn to Mrs. Salina who will demonstrate how a transformation of a traumatic psychological self-portrait can be achieved in a psychobiographic approach.

CHAPTER EIGHTEEN

Person Studies: Mrs. Salina, Nick, Alma

In the beginning phases of establishing the relationship I am concerned with negotiating power vectors through minimization of (1) the fear of pathography, and (2) the sense of defeat. The ultimate conversion of the sense of defeat to a sense of hope, and eventually victory, is being achieved through a gradual mutual depiction (i.e., remembering) of different life experiences, whose relative saliency is determined again by mutual exploration, and the fitting of those experiences into the rubric of one's development (and not only psychological development).

It is important to notice that the relative importance of an event, like the meaning attached to it, is determined through the meeting and by the Other as the ultimate validator. The Other, to remind you, is everyone, not only Freud, Jung, Rogers, Allport, and so-and-so. The person, any person, refreshing our memory, is their own playwright.

Biographic interpretation is grounded in experience, in life. It is always event-bounded, reflecting on the uniqueness of the never recurring event, and the acting characters. It is ever unique, never universal. It is always in a process of transformation; shaping and reshaping like a person's life. Psychobiography comprises biography + affect + meaning; biographic interpretation involves the affect and the meaning aspects. While the biography, a particular event or stream of events, once reconstructed, essentially remains the same, the affects and the meaning(s) attached to the events change with the ever-changing person. Though the person is the one who confers meaning, the centerpiece is the event, or the occurrence, itself. The meaning and the attached affect change as the event reshapes itself, supplied with additional information and detail. Initially, it is the event that implies affective responses and meaning attachments. One child may respond with depression to their parents' divorce, another with mild functional sadness, and another with relief. Apparently, it seems that the same event elicits different affective responses, but not so, since what elicits the different responses is the context which comprises what precedes and what succeeds the act of divorce. The act of divorce is the basic unit, the event. A set of basic interrelated units comprise the context. A person in context confers meaning(s) and affects.

Here are the four possibilities of the interplay of the person–event context:

1. The person is aware of the event but not the context.
2. The person is aware of both the event and the context.
3. The person is not aware of the event (as for the context—unknown).
4. The person is not aware of either. Total amnesia.

In the first instance, there is a vague memory of the occurrence: a man remembers he traveled in 1977. The affective response is constricted and general: "It was good." It is a single noncontextual, and maybe also dissociated, occurrence. It may or may not have saliency.

In the second, the person is generally aware of both the context and the event. A person knows what anticipated the occurrence, what was responsible for it, and what the consequences were. The person can potentially relate to affects and meanings he or she has assigned to it. There is a possibility of omissions of important details which may or may not have impact on the affects and meaning(s), as well as a possibility for alternative meaning(s) and affective transformation.

In the third instance an important event, usually traumatic, with its accompanying affects and meaning(s), has been suppressed and dissociated from awareness.

The fourth represents deeply fragmented personal histories. Lois falls somewhere in between 3 and 4.

In what will follow here, I shall provide some examples which illustrate how a combination of biographic questions, biographic disclosure, and biographic interpretation results in transformation of experience and a shift upward in the interplay between person, event, and context toward integration of different events into a person's life story, thereby augmenting (i.e., associating) the person's experiential space.

X: *How are you today?*
Y: *I am okay.*
X: *Did you get used to the cold?*
Y: *I am trying to but still find it difficult.*
X: *Are you from a warm country?*
Y: *Yes, how about you?*
X: *I am, too.*

Y: *Are you used to the cold?*

X: *Yes, now it is okay.*

Y: *Now, in contrast to when?*

X: *When I first came here.*

Y: *When?*

X: *I have lived here now for almost X years.*

Y: *Time has done its job.*

X: *Yes.*

Y: *You know, when I first came here after a few days I went shopping alone and entered a pretty big supermarket only to find myself racing through the aisles and after 2 minutes I was out, empty-handed, looking at the sky. I needed something familiar to ground myself. I didn't even know what a bottle of milk looked like.*

X: *Did you have family here?*

Y: *Yes.*

X: *I didn't even have that. I took a cab from the airport to a friend of my mother's whom I didn't know. I felt strange.*

Before I continue, review the above excerpt: can you tell who is who? It could have been me and you talking to each other, enjoying our mutual companionship and a hot, aromatic cup of tea. How compassionate a companionship might be!

Mrs. Salina

X is Mrs. Salina, a middle-aged Hispanic woman who at the age of 19 immigrated to the United States, leaving behind her whole poor family. Her parents had separated when she was 12, and the nine children were divided between the parents. She first lived with her mother, then her father, and then with her mother

again before she traveled again this time to the unknown, finding herself married and living with an unknown man—at only 19 years of age plus a few months.
This era of her life lasted for no less than 25 years—long
years of holding a full-time job while raising two children and providing for another, hormonally grown-up
child (her husband) who used to intimidate her on a
daily basis, cursing at her, spending his time with
friends, drinking alcoholic beverages bought with his
wife's earnings, and sharing their bed with other
women. She was enslaved. Did she have a part in that?
You do remember: what is outside is inside, they say.
Well, that is exactly what *she* says. A few years ago she
managed to separate from him. Since then she has been
severely depressed, living out of no choice with a son
and daughter-in-law, and though she knows she did the
right thing, nevertheless, she still believes she should
have put up with her marriage and blames herself for
not doing so: "I miss his presence, not him," is the way
she voices her merciless loneliness.

Though we were able to establish a relationship, I
was bothered with the paucity of biographical content
she was able to share. She would answer my biographical
prompts with short, factual, and affectless statements,
until the above biographical disclosure by *Me.* She was
able to integrate a factual and vaguely remembered
occurrence into a historical context, filling the gaps
(omissions), fully experiencing its meanings and its
emotional implications.

She knew only a few words in English when she arrived in the United States, and dined a stranger, at the
table of her mother's friend. Why didn't she work? "I
didn't have permission to work," she answers as a matter
of fact. Then she was introduced by the lady stranger to

her would-be husband. She understood the hint: you are getting to be too much. She felt the walls were closing in on her, and feared she would find herself in the streets. She married him. She didn't love him, but he was likable, and treated her well, and she thought she would learn to love him. "And you needed the green card," I say. Salina cried. Tears of shame. Was she so desperate? Why didn't she go back home? There should be a home to go back to, right? There wasn't one for her. Her mother was never married to her father, she said; she actually had two "husbands," married to neither. Her mother gave birth to 11 children, two of whom died at birth. Mother either was indifferent or extremely demanding, while the father was easy in using his leather belt so faithfully that "it left signs on the skin." She had no place to go back to. Her flight to America, we agreed, was of double meaning. In marrying she was trying to survive. "I gave myself a chance," she said, bringing to a conclusion the interpretation of a piece of her own biography.

One day, shortly before the termination of our meetings, Mrs. Salina turned to me saying: "Now I know I gave myself a second chance," referring to her leaving her husband. Why a second? "When I married him! Then, have you forgotten?" she replied. She was not to be blamed any more. What was outside remained outside: shame.

Mrs. Salina confirms that "we can know more than we can tell" (Polanyi, 1983, p. 4), and that the act of a therapeutic discourse is an act of empowerment of each, one at a time, to put into words what one has already experienced, thus unfolding the unknown.

Mrs. Salina now had a story, not a fragmented-dissociated piece of a story, a meteor-like occurrence cruising unguided in an infinite space. She came to understand that her life had a sense to it, that, after all, she was a, and the, continuity in an ever-changing and overwhelming world, and that she was an active playwright of it, not just a germ of dust whipped away by a man's belt, another's curse, and a woman's coldness.

Nick

As a transition, I would like to demonstrate the difference between a psychoanalytic and a biographic interpretation. It was told to me by a friend and colleague who thought I might have some interest in it.

Nick, a pseudonym, like all the Others' names, was working with a young man who confronted great difficulties in talking about having been several times sexually abused in preadolescence. Each session another piece of the abuse was being unfolded until it came to a point where Nick felt the man was close to getting in touch with his pain. During the next session with his supervisor, Nick talked about meeting pain, not his, but another's. He said it was not easy for him to witness another's pain even if it was for the 100th time. "He told me there is no growth without pain, what a revelation, and that it is something about me, would you believe that, countertransference, and that maybe I have difficulties being sadistic. I sure do. . . ."

The question is not if it was a good or bad interpretation. You may phrase it as you may wish. We are not talking cosmetics but substance, to which I referred elsewhere. Now I want to focus on how a psychobiographic person therapist would approach the same episode. First, you want to remember that Nick is the site of knowledge; second, that we are in a mutual endeavor. Instead of focusing on "you," on the intrapsychic, a psychobiographer focuses on the event, in this case an interpersonal event: the context of Nick feeling the pain of the Other's living. This of course is an existential, and not a Freudian, pain. First, and foremost, pain entails empathy, recalling Rogers, and in any case the object of pain should be addressed regarding its nature. A historically oriented psychobiographer may inquire about other cases in which Nick was involved either as a witness or as a victim. A series of biographic questions always precedes any potential biographical interpretation. Biographical interpretation, and interpretation in general, as already suggested by Rogers, is not unavoidable. In any event, it is always being generated through a process in the same way as a symphony by Beethoven gradually builds up into its peaks. No matter with whom you orchestrate it, alone or mutually with the Other, to be effective, an interpretation in a therapeutic meeting is always a process, an experience. In the above case, Nick just needed someone to share with.

Alma

Now I turn to another example where the event has been entirely dissociated, losing the very reason why the dissociation was employed in the first place: its meaning(s) and accompanying affect(s). We have already met Alma (p. 165). Once she came in very much concerned about her daughter's pending marriage. She remembered her own marriage and felt guilty that she could not give her daughter a palatial wedding ceremony such as her own parents had been able to give her.

There was such a distortion in her belief system that there might be, though I recommend otherwise, a temptation to confront her cognitive "all or nothing" or her splitting style. But apart from telling her something she already knew but could not resist, and thus belittle her self-esteem, we would have lost important information. Being aware that personal sharing means intimacy, I made a judgment that the timing was right and opted for a biographical disclosure. I told Alma that I had been married twice and each time it was a very simple ceremony. "Oh," she replied, and I was very glad that she was sitting down, "you were married twice!" and she changed the subject abruptly. A couple of minutes later a dissociated memory flew into the session: "Now I remember my husband was married before he married me; he had two children from her. I always wondered why he was so good to her but not to me." The memory generated so many shameful, thus painful, feel-ings—not only of a mistreating and discriminating (i.e., humiliating) husband but also the mere status of being a divorcee, and having married a divorcee—that she had just pushed away, suppressed, and dissociated the feelings from the event. At one point I asked her:

Me: *How did you come to remember this now?*

She: *Probably what you said about yourself.*

Me: *You seemed in shock to me.*

She: *Did I?* [She smiled a bemused smile.] *I don't know, maybe I am not used to . . . I don't know, I was caught off guard.*

Me: *And this is not something you are used to?*

She: *No, no, no, in our family we know what to expect. . . .*

Me: *Not so much with your husband* [an explosive alco-holic]. . . .

She: *Oh, he gave me a hard time but I knew him, he was easy to read even when he exploded, I could tell.* [Beware of the temptation to interpret *her* actions, or *her* part in these episodes, for first, we do not know the full context with its complexities: maybe she just didn't have a part, and, second, we will empower, at this junction, her helplessness: "I collaborated. Therefore, I am bad, too."]

Me: *Was there anybody in your family not so easy to read?*

She: *You mean my daughters or . . .?*

Me: *Say, your mother.*

She: *She is kind of* [with an affectionate voice] *old fashioned.* [Her voice changes.] *She is complicated, private.*

Me: *Secrets. . . .*

She: *Oh, so much! I tell her* [angry voice], *"Mom, how come everybody knows but me?" and she says she thought it's not so important or something like that.*

Me: *How do you feel then?*

She: *It's not fair.*

Me: *It sure is not; how do you feel when it happens?*

She: *I feel pushed aside . . . hiding from me . . .* [long pause] *it's a shame . . . I feel shame . . . what is wrong with me that they hide from me . . .?*

Me: *I think* [I changed the modus purposefully inviting her to take up an interpreting-clarifying process to make some sense of shame in her life] *you were talking about giving; what is giving? You mentioned your parents giving you a nice ceremony and you felt ashamed because you can't afford the same kind of giving with your own daughter, and you might have been wondering if you were a good mother. Then you mentioned your husband giving to her but not to you, and your mother not giving you—what?*

She: *It's closeness . . . when you told me about yourself I didn't know what to do with that, how I should take*

> *it . . . do you understand what I am saying* [very confused]?

Me: *I understand that you said you would like to know what intimacy is, what is give-and-take in a close relationship* [= unlearning], *is that correct?*

To sum up, we notice again the interplay of biographic questions, biographic disclosure, and biographic interpretation in eliciting dissociated feelings and meanings. I attached the feeling to its biographical event/context and by way of doing that within an interpersonal experiential context it became specified, nongeneralized, and contextual, and thus amenable to control and change. In the psychobiographic approach Me strives to help Other to identify not only the feeling but also its context: identify the feeling + identify its event-related history.

Pay attention to how a timely biographical self-disclosure served not only the moment, but also a developmental deprivation: anonymity and thus vagueness = nondemarcated, nongiving parental figure.

The interpersonal relationship between Me and Other never serves itself but only the process. People are coming to Me to get help to lead a better life, whatever better may imply, or in Sullivan's words, to cope better with "problems in living." The experience of Me-Other should always serve this end. Accordingly, the reciprocity always and ultimately ends with the Other and for the benefit of the Other. The person studies above demonstrate these provisions when Me ventures back and forth with the interpersonal, here-and-now, and here-and-there, and ultimately ends up with implications for the Other's day-to-day present life.

We leave archaeology for archaeologists, history per se for historians, yet live psychohistorical biography, according to what one man, noted for his biography, had to say: "... in general people experience their present naively, as it were, without being able to form an estimate of its contents; they have first to put themselves at a distance from it—the present, that is to say, must have become the past—before it can yield points of vantage from which to judge the future" (Freud, 1927/1962, p. 5).

The question is: to which past are we attuned? The question carries part of the answer, provided we make a slight but meaningful correction: to which past is a psychobiographer attuned? The psychobiographic approach, being a mutual and egalitarian interaction, does not dictate a preference of any one developmental stage over another. Such an approach lets the "data" speak and determine what the events were that occurred at what developmental stages contributed to the Other's personality formation. For Mrs. Salina it was her late adolescence; and Alma was much preoccupied with events during her preadolescence. The relative weight of early experiences changes with age. It may happen that 10 years later Mrs. Salina may find more interest in happenings in her early childhood. Much of my professional choice had to do with experiences during my adolescence, but the character of my professional practice, once I made the choice, was influenced from experiences during my early childhood. The principle of universality does not have a grip in reality either between people or within people.

CHAPTER NINETEEN

Person Studies: Mark, Harry

Earlier I mentioned a turning point along the continuum of I–thou relationships where the impersonal becomes personal and the Other decides to take the risk of giving Me a position of power. This actually symbolizes an important shift in the process and in the power structure of psychotherapy. In one form or another the Other says something like, "Before now I felt compelled to come here and now I feel I am coming because I want to." This decision is being made under the premise that Me is sincere-nonjudgmental, fair-nonmanipulative, possesses integrity-nonexploiting, and is a wise-nonpathographizer, otherwise therapy will either terminate prematurely with no meaningful results, but with the pretense of having been effective (depending on the therapist's ability to write down preformulated "goals achieved" and "objectives achieved"), or it may last infinitely, playing on a theme named "power struggle" with at least economically definitive results. In one case, therapy has been just an incident, a meaningless event that soon will fade, while in the other case it becomes an ongoing tragedy: yet another trauma.

A psychobiographic approach is always short-term but with long-term effects. The Other is being told that entering what is called in lay language "therapy," is nothing more than entering college, learning about life—that psychology is about life. In this particular college we learn about your life; it is exclusively for you, to

239

make sense out of your own life. You are actually writing your own biography, your story. I will share with you my experience of your story and my experience with psychology; I will accompany you as your assisting psychobiographer. Together we will write the preface to your biography, and as soon as we are done you may go and continue your autobiography, chapter after chapter. You may come back to me, or to another, for a visit or two when you feel your pen is out of ink.

Usually the duration of the meetings depends on mutual negotiation and agreement. When there is no alternative I may note 20 sessions as advisable; then I always add the possibility of earlier termination if the Other chooses it, provided that I am told beforehand that we will be able to discuss the issue. As people differ from one another in terms of their needs, to designate a number will be arbitrary and likely to content only commercial ears. From my experience I usually foresee somewhere between 8 months and 2 years.

Shorter terms of psychotherapy have come into the market, exactly for that reason, to market, and as such they are not of interest to us. It is my conviction that these therapies (the term now is so well suited) have a factor in common with the other, longer therapies they oppose and claim to replace.

First, let me state, if what I have done so far does not suffice, what I think went wrong with those long-term psychotherapies (LTP). They are power-oriented, according to the definitions I suggested here. They manipulate the relationship but do not get into being *in* a relationship. The interpersonal experience is negative, disempowering, perpetuating itself. No wonder that therapy goes on and on. Some advocates of short-term psychotherapy (STP) believe that therapy goes on and on because many people have problems with separation-individuation and therefore when the therapeutic alliance has been established between the two, that famous, mysterious "click," then therapy continues endlessly and terminates only when one of them dies or because of some other external circumstance. Therefore, they say, we should impose a time limit.

What these STPs advocate is simple: eliminate the, in their language, "click"—no attachments, no bonding, nothing interpersonal, no experience in I-thou. These, they say, have proved to be ineffective. But pay attention carefully: who proved that? The person therapist! We, therefore, need STP because of our professional and especially personal limitations. We need to invent a technique in order to disguise our personal defects: our inability to separate and individuate. We then believe that a technique will do that for . . . *them*. What a tragic mistrust of us and them!

Going back to our LTPs, the STPs are perfectly right, not in their answer to the predicament, but in their protest against it. They should also learn to point their blaming fingers toward the right object, refraining from projections: the therapists. I asked a colleague who had been in psychoanalytic therapy for 10 years, four sessions a week during the first years and fewer in later years, when she thought it would be done, and she said, with an expression of awe and holiness on her face and in her voice: "My analyst says I will be ready in 6 months." She had no comments on my inquiry about her own opinion.

The LTPs and STPs have a factor in common: both are techniques, giving rise to a person who is not capable of establishing rapport. The first actually engages itself in a one-up, one-down relationship in the name of the Other's well-being; the second, fearful of any relationship that may lead to dependency and exploitation, gives up any attempt at genuine and real (non-technical) human rapport (and adjusts, conforms, to the market trend).

A psychobiographic approach that emphasizes a unique interpersonal experience facilitates rapport and hence shortens the length of therapy, thereby decreasing human suffering.

According to the principle of reciprocity advocated here, apart from inability or difficulties in establishing rapport, the two parties may also be afflicted with another affliction: idealization. The psychobiographic approach refrains from pathographizing as well as idealizing. I am not referring to the well-known mythology of a golden age of childhood, or the faultless family, a mythology so typically held by many millions of people in the closed and open wards. Volumes have been written about the place of mythology and ideal images in human evolution; here I need to stress a particular meaning of idealization as it is embedded in the practice of psychotherapy.

Idealization is a borrowed concept, imported into psychology like many others. Actually it is a sociopolitical concept, and either way it means *not real, false*. The idea of falsehood is embedded in many other terms and synonyms such as: as if, persona, image, faked, mask, etc. Why do we need to idealize, and who needs it? The answer seems obvious as far as psychotherapy is concerned. The borderline–narcissistic splitting serves as a dramatic prototype of pathological idealization; the patient, it is generally assumed, idealizes and devaluates, him or herself and others to the same extent, and at any rate is the source of the idealization, generating their own psychopathology. In other words, again, what is outside is inside, and the patient is again made responsible for the genesis of their own internal state, making themselves sick, traumatizing themselves. Accordingly, psychotherapy claims, we should "adjust" the patient either by fixing distorted (i.e., idealized) beliefs (cf, cognitive and other "reality"-oriented therapies), or by analyzing unconscious idealized–internalized self-objects.

A psychobiographic approach postulates that idealization emanates from a pathological sociopolitical reality endorsed by others, as well as the Other, in order to "adjust" to the same unbearable oppressive reality. Facades of greatness have become the hidden message behind any cultural product. Industrialism has just further disseminated and elaborated on a theme that forever served as a tool for distraction from social discontent, manipulation by intensifying dreams of glory and fame, and consequently a tool for control. This image of greatness led some, in the 1980s, to believe that we are living in a narcissistic society (Lasch, 1979), and others, just a few years later in the 1990s, in a borderline society (Kreisman & Straus, 1989). We may encounter a psychotic society if idealizations (i.e., distortions) of our nature as simply human beings, keep flourishing and further disintegrating our personal and social personalities. Psychotherapies contribute to this state of disintegration by disseminating the same culturally defined tools of power: facades of expertism and greatness.

I turn again to the practice of the psychobiographic approach and see how practically it counters this social power tool. What I will say here, like what I have said before, should not be treated separately from what has been said throughout this book.

Mark

Mark, a 32-year-old single man, insisted on calling me "Doc," despite my appeals. He apparently needed to preserve a distance between us and keep my image impersonal and inhuman (i.e., idealized). What better idea for excusing an unwillingness to commit to therapy? After numerous hospitalizations, following acute paranoid ideation and suicidal attempts, he still needed vigorous persuasion to comply with medication. When released from the last hospitalization he agreed to "talking" with a therapist and was referred to an outpatient clinic.

Talking is my profession—as are said "talking cures," at least sometimes—and since Mark declared, "I do not have any problem," and since, as you may imagine, I agreed with him, and since we both love Italian food, we talked about Italian food. We were not in agreement about whose lasagna would win a cooking contest, but ultimately we acclaimed the virtues of diversity—but not so much concerning other issues as concerning cooking.

To wit, Mark obstinately believed that a person of exalted rank should graduate from a four-year college. Mark's romance with "college" contained many facets, including both inferior and grandiose self-allegations concerning his intelligence (intelligence complex), and his complicated relationship with his father, but it was also an expression of a conventional would be ideal self-image he had internalized and considered as a symbol of success and *power.* He made it clear that the last hypothesis was something he was both concerned and half-hearted about. And we "worked" on that: I gradually demystified the alleged facade of the expert's cult: I was just a chum (Didn't he agree to "talk" to someone?). There is simply a person behind a P-h-D, he was asked to observe. We were delighted to read excerpts I carefully selected from biographies that exposed hidden truths about the prestigious and the eminent. We found the story about a callous ruler who got a Ph.D. from one of the most prestigious universities, by commanding it, as very sad and discouraging in terms of the condition of science as well as humanity, but that intelligence and corruption may dwell under the same roof—this fact was not overlooked, along with the many faces of power.

One day Mark greeted me, I noticed, not as usual. "Hello, Mr. Yerushalmi," I heard him say. Two months later he was participating in a psychiatric rehabilitation program.

Idealizations contain a potentially healthy seed to which *Me* should pay close attention. In any idealization one finds a need, deprived, and a wish, to be fulfilled. Mark idealized intellectual achievement out of a need to be truly respected as a man who has a say, and out of a wish for meaning and power. When I left the clinic, Mark was still playing with the idea of entering college, and he was encouraged to do so! People need a cause to live for and even if that ideal is unattainable, it is desirable as long as it leads the way to day-by-day living and does not divert the mind from it. We all need more than one dream to keep on living.

The process of deprofessionalization and hence rehumanization and demystification of psychotherapy involves, then, a relationship at a nonidealized human level.

Harry

Another example will help to further elucidate potential pitfalls of idealization. Harry had lived a pretty successful life when he called and asked for an appointment. The brief telephone interview did not yield any clue as to the reasons for his appealing for help now. When asked what I could do for him, he answered, "I am not sure; I do not feel at rest," and denied that this feeling had anything to do with his recent divorce. What followed was an in-depth exercise in the revival of an emotional history, and it lasted for three years. Harry had been forced to leave his parents at a young age; meanwhile, the father died, and Harry was left wondering who his father really was and what his attitude toward him had been. History being contextual, we needed to revive the events themselves; some of them he remembered, but he was not sure of his recollections; others he was able to collect from family reminiscences, but then again he was not sure of his family's recollections either. Life history being in part written history, I asked him for documents. It happened that he and his father were in pretty intense correspondence for the first three years after their separation. And Harry had a short diary that contained ostensibly very factual information about his first four days after the separation, and upon request he could also furnish a dozen or so family pictures. It was a most fascinating journey into the history of emotions and meanings for an individual struggling with bitterness when facing uncertainties of double meaning and ambiguous happenings, and when facing painful truths and then reconciling with the unavoidable. He, we together, asked the data questions: Why is his diary so short? What kind of a person is emerging out of these writings? Where is the actual and real, and where is the "would like to be"? What is the emotional tone and does it match the one he remembers before his departure? How did his father portray himself, and how can we portray him? Is there any "central underlying story" (McAdams, 1988, p. 2) that animates his father's life? Where is the mother? Why is she relatively absent and her role subordinate to that of the father? How do his siblings fit into the emerging picture?

Harry was discovering that he was not an event, a free-floating meteor, but a series of events with a historical unity deriving from the past and continuing into the future. He read the brilliant book *Letters from Jenny* (Allport, 1965), and he made further explorations into personalities with *Lives in Progress* (White, 1975), and some excerpts from Tomkins' scripts.

From a traditional point of view, Harry might have been treated with some sort of cost-effective short-term therapy for depression. The goal-setter expert/therapist might have decided that Harry's divorce might have triggered a reactive nonpsychotic depression which would call for some sort of time-limited cognitive or interpersonal or dynamic rehabilitation. Yet another alternative might have been a long-term archaeological excavation into the deeper layers of Harry without his historical context but with his fantasies.

In a psychobiographic approach, as has been noted, the Other explores and sets the goal mutually with Me. This process itself is of critical importance for the well-being of a person, who, like me and you, must learn for their own benefit to ask the right questions and look for the right answers by and for themselves, and by providing the questions and then the preconceived "scientific" answers, we are actually doing harm.

Harry demonstrates for me, first, what I have advocated here, that, "We must study a personality not only the long way developmentally, but also the deep way biologically and the broad way historically" (Tomkins, 1987, p. 147), unless one assumes that the personality of a person-in-psychotherapy is so tainted with psychopathology that different forms of study should be applied to him or her. This last assumption was challenged by me, since I advocate the same approach for all.

Second, Harry demonstrates the usefulness of personal documents in learning about oneself. At one point or another, considering appropriate timing, I ask the Other to bring me a dozen or so family pictures, which yield a host of information, such as the emotional atmosphere in the family, the relative position of the family members to each other as a reflection of role importance, omissions of members vis-à-vis overrepresentation, and the like.

The use of documents should blend naturally into the I–thou relationship. Documents should be relinquished if they serve as a means of distancing ourselves from each other—if use of them becomes a technique. I usually offer a self-help book I have read myself and suggest that later we may exchange impressions, or if I have not read the book I ask to be informed and taught about it. The timing of this kind of giving is also important because any act of giving might be interpreted in several very diverse ways, and I would like the Other to know I care about his or her feelings in this particular case, as well as in any case.

I also use biographies and autobiographies that dramatically exemplify a theme in living. Beethoven's struggle with a disability and his resolution of the question of life and death as unfolded in a magnificent letter

(Solomon, 1977) assists me with people who have the same concerns. A professor's struggle with manic-depression (Jamison, 1993) is another example. I usually choose biographies that refrain from self- and other-glorification and portray a character on a human level. Great figures' weaknesses and foibles humanize our condition as well as, at times, very much amuse us. Most meaningful is the mere act of offering a biography that serves as an invitation to a mutual exploration of a life to be continued by the person.

Documents also serve another substantial issue in understanding one's life: depicting the atmosphere of the era. What was the prevailing mode of socioeconomical thinking, values, and morality at the time of the actual happening? What is the broad historical context?

In 1971, Guntrip, a representative of the culture of his time, says: "In short, we have now arrived at the time when it is apparent that man's major problem is not how to understand and master his universal physical environment but to understand himself and find out how we can help one another to live truly self- and other-fulfilling lives" (p. 147).

Twenty years later, in the era of "disposable" people (Castro, 1993), Bloom (1993) says: "Human evolution has geared us for survival, not for satisfaction, pleasure, self-actualization, or higher consciousness" (p. 266).

As this is the more practical section of my work, I will put aside the broader question of how culture affects psychotherapy and how it is, or whether it is, affected by it. Let me make it clear that I am suggesting not this or that psychotherapeutic disposition, but a historical study of the person in their (and not your prevailing wisdom's) historical context. The historical moment of happening confers meaning on the happening and not any external, artificially imposed meaning. In a broad sense I referred to this subject in the first section of my work. Here I want to emphasize a specific case which comes to further anchor psychotherapy in history—in the meaning of practices (e.g., child rearing, general attitude toward I-thou, family practices, etc.) at the time of the happening. Consider the following:

A man in his 40s tells me: "When she approached to beat me with the stick I grabbed it forcefully and pushed her and threw her on the floor." At that time he was 8 years old, and the mother in her late 20s. What was the meaning of her behavior? For us in the 1990s her behavior is self-evident, but if we interpret this piece of behavior from our era's value system then we may be adding salt to the wound of our 40-year-old child. I am not saying that the mother's behavior should be justified but merely that in order to tap the intricacies of behavior and as a consequence the subtleties of emotions involved, we should familiarize ourselves with the value system of the happening's era. This can be delineated by taking an oral history from relatives, or by referring to journals, articles, and books from the era. Many times we will discover that social, economic, and political trends contain a better explanation than intrapsychic explanations, and a more exact one, and this is what is important.

I have met so many expert/therapists who plunge into the "real" motivations for changing a job, moving, or doing this or the other thing, only to find that a recession was on the horizon or termites invaded the neighborhood. Let us turn now to another invader: poverty.

I will not undertake the task of providing you with dry and yet overwhelming statistics about poverty; I assume that as a person well-versed in life you know the facts anyway. There are, of course, vast layers of disenfranchised people, in inner and outer cities. The decent wage jobs continue to decline and with them the equitable distribution of wealth. In a study of 23 people with long lives of exceptional moral commitment and contributions in vast areas of society, the largest number concerned themselves with poverty (Colby, 1994).

I am using this as an introduction to the last part of my work—last but not least, as it is really only the beginning. Trauma is oppression, and trauma happens in an oppression-prone society.

A psychobiographic approach strives to help the person not only to recognize the current social dilemmas and values, as suggested previously but also to recognize the current social oppressors in their own experience. Here I am referring to the more general cultural oppressors that breed the conditions for the more personal immediate oppressors; a culture that is indifferent to the agony of its children, adolescents, and adults, thus perpetuating victimization from generation to generation.

The course of history is governed by economic necessity. This is not just a Marxian premise, though Marx voiced it, but the fundamental premise of the Western "bottom line" society. Those who benefit from it are those who are deaf toward its victims as they are toward any cultural analysis. For them, change is change in attitudes, whether cognitively or dynamically construed. The dehumanization process owes its genesis to the denial and oppression of the fact that only culture can confer psychological identity and only culture can take it away.

Most astonishing and illuminating is the indifference of a privileged class, the lack of interest in economic factors in the life course of a person. Throughout my long and diverse professional experience with nurses, social workers, psychologists, and psychiatrists I have not met even a single person who has taken a thorough economic history of the person. And I wonder how many protests have been passed by unheard.

As suffering is embedded in sociopolitical reality, so is redemption in social action. A psychobiographically oriented person helps another person to transform their personal protest into a personally meaningful social protest—and action. The journey ends when this transformation has been achieved to the degree defined by the person's readiness to put at risk their natural endowments and willingness. And it is only the beginning.

CHAPTER TWENTY

The Psychobiographic Approach: Summary of Principles

- The guild of professional psychotherapists, by the nature of its practices and the kinds of affiliations it has with current economic–political–social systems, perpetuates the human misery it purports to remedy. It further objectifies a person who has been objectified either by others or by life, or both. It abuses the abused. It collaborates with the prevailing social system in converting the misery inflicted *upon* the person to misery inflicted *from within* the person.

- Current psychotherapy is a microcosm of an authoritarian and oppressive sociopolitical reality in which the weak and needy are created and manufactured and then exploited under the guise of a benevolent technicoscientific procedure. For the macro, as well as the micro, the values of money, consumption, and objectifying have permeated the basic unit of relationship and thus the whole domain of living.

- Society is ill. Our culture is what is sick.

- A person resorts to therapy, which is conceived as enemy, by force (e.g., of symptoms, spouse's complaint, civil institutions, etc.) and not by will. It is conceived as defeat due to pathographizing processes. Nevertheless, the mere act of resorting to therapy reflects and symbolizes a protest and a wish;

253

the detection and mobilization of this protest is at
the core of the therapeutic interaction.

- In order for psychotherapy to serve its true purpose
  of impoverishment of alienation it should dissociate
  itself from its historical alliance with a failing educational system and from the medical model.

- A separatist, nonegalitarian attitude is a reflection
  of the power structure of psychotherapy. The separatist, power-oriented, person elitist/therapist uses
  placebo rituals, anonymity (or disclosure) of themselves and their technique or both, usurpation of the
  role of the knower from the other person, pathographizing processes, and manipulation of the unconscious, and of relationship and belief systems. In
  psychobiography we are engaged in abolishing these
  power ingredients.

- Psychobiography is being proposed in response to a
  power structure transferred from society to the
  realm of a unique person-to-person meeting labeled
  as psychotherapy. Power is at the core of any human
  interaction, including psychotherapy.

- Psychobiography addresses the myth of separatism
  which stems from a collective fear of madness, of
  being different and therefore outcast from the humane and human race; it thus humanizes mental
  suffering and distress. Madness is embedded in human nature.

- In psychobiography the Other, and not the expert-
  therapist, is the source of knowledge, both intellectual and emotional. You are the knower. You are the
  primary source. I need you as well as you need me
  in order to make sense of your life in light of your
  biography. Psychobiography is the craft of helping

the Other experience what that person already knows.

- Resistance in therapy more often than not reflects an implicit yet actual power component present in the meeting, in the therapist's personality, or both. Resistance in the process of therapy might actually reflect a resistance on the part of the therapist to check for overreliance on technical maneuvers hiding behind the "expert" self.

- In psychobiography the Other's reality is trusted, his or her reality is real. This trust implies respect and is the basis for a real, trustworthy meeting, as opposed to imposed and at times even faked–manufactured trust practiced in current psychotherapies.

- Indifference is yet another form of objectifying processes, or trauma.

- People need to be aware of their oppressors. Most people do not have this awareness, and if they do they are unable to deal with it appropriately, that is, to their own satisfaction. It has been argued here that our profession at times is a contributor to and not a remedy for abuse, and that the Other is persuaded to believe in the latter. Psychobiography is cued toward detection and unfolding of oppressive traumatic factors in the practice of psychotherapy, as well as in the social milieu.

- The Other is the one who, together with the psychobiographer, sets the aim of each and every meeting. The Other is the one who makes the decision, pertaining to what "remedies" are "curative" for him or her. That moment of choice encompasses a proposition for a biographical approach toward the person's existence. From that moment we are dealing with a biographer assisted in his or her inquiries by a psychobiographer.

- Mobilization of the faculties of intuition and asking questions, two faculties among others which have been suppressed by the formal educational processes, are at the core of the psychobiographic approach.

- Meaning, from its lower side of the median aiming at "us" and from the upper side—as "I"—is perceived as the right answer to the question of life.

- Psychobiography is historically conscious. It recognizes in its practice the impact of the "structure of feeling" of an era on the minutae of everyday life and on the stream of events during development.

- Psychobiography adheres to creative synthesis of current pertinent psychological knowledge, including psychopathological theory, but especially developmental psychology and nonpathographizing personality theories.

- The state of existence being as it is, dissociation is a humane and necessary process. We encounter psychological distress when dissociative processes are massively utilized as a consequence of massive objectifying processes.

- Psychobiography's time agency is three-dimensional, consisting of past-present-future.

- The psychobiographer offers biographical interpretations-insights while he or she is attuned to the Other's biographical time.

- The psychobiographer offers a meeting which functions as an alimentary symbiosis and in which the psychobiographer is fully demarcated, offering understanding, warmth, genuineness, acceptance, nonpossessiveness, and his or her psychobiography.

- Psychobiography aims at (1) the felt helplessness of the Other in face of life and its objectifying processes, and (2) making the encounter an experience of primal quality: lack of power exertion.
- Idealization is conceived as yet another power maneuver utilized for exerting control, depriving others of autonomous thinking, and dehumanizing life.

References

Abramson, P. R. (1992). *A case for case studies: An immigrant's journal.* Newbury Park, CA: Sage.

Africa, T. W. (1979). Psychohistory, ancient history, and Freud: The descent into Avernus. *Arethusa, 12*(1), 5 33.

Alexander, I. E. (1990). *Personology: Method and content in personality assessment and psychobiography.* Durham, NC: Duke University Press.

Allende, I. (1985). *The house of the spirits.* New York: Bantam.

Allport, G. W. (1961). *Pattern and growth in personality.* New York: Holt, Rinehart & Winston.

Allport, G. W. (1965). *Letters from Jenny.* New York: Harcourt, Brace & World.

Allport, G. W. (1968). *The person in psychology: Selected essays.* Boston: Beacon Press.

Anderson, H., & Goolishian, H. A. (1988). Human systems as linguistic systems: Preliminary and evolving ideas about the implications for clinical theory. *Family Process, 27*(4), 371–393.

Armstrong, L. (1978). *Kiss Daddy goodnight: A speak-out on incest.* New York: Hawthorn Books.

Beck, A. T. (Speaker). (1990). *Cognitive therapy of an avoidant personality* (Cassette Recording No. 2966). New York: Guilford.

Beck, A. T., Rush, A. J., Shaw, B. F., & Emery, G. (1979). *Cognitive therapy of depression.* New York: Guilford.

Becker, C. L. (1932). Everyman his own historian. *American Historical Review, 37,* 221–236.

Behr, C. (1994). *Final assignment.* Unpublished manuscript, New York University, School of Social Work.

Bergin, A. E., & Strupp, H. H. (1972). *Changing frontiers in the science of psychotherapy.* Chicago: Aldine Atherton.

Bloom, S. L. (1993). The clinical uses of psychohistory. *The Journal of Psychohistory, 20*(3), 259–266.

Boring, E. G. (1957). *A history of experimental psychology* (2nd ed.). New York: Appleton Century Crofts.

Boring, E. G., & Lindzey, G. (Eds.). (1952). *A history of psychology in autobiography* (Vol. 4). New York: Russell & Russell.

Brehm, J. W. (1966). *A theory of psychological reactance.* New York: Academic Press.

Brehm, S. S., & Brehm, J. W. (1981). *Psychological reactance: A theory of freedom and control.* New York: Academic Press.

Brown, R. (1995, May/June). Columbo therapy. *Networker,* 42–44.

Bruner, J. (1986). *Actual minds, possible worlds.* Cambridge, MA: Harvard University Press.

Bruner, J. (1990). *Acts of meaning.* Cambridge, MA: Harvard University Press.

Buber, M. (1958). *I and Thou.* New York: Collier Books.

Bugental, J. F. T. (1987). *The art of the psychotherapist.* New York: W. W. Norton.

Burns, D. D. (1980). *Feeling good: The new mood therapy.* New York: Signet.

Cartwright, A. K. J. (1981). Are different therapeutic perspectives important in the treatment of alcoholism? *British Journal of Addiction, 76,* 347–361.

Castro, J. (1993, March 29). Disposable workers. *Time, 141*(13), 42–47.

Cohen, D. (1977). *Psychologists on psychology.* London: Routledge & Kegan Paul.

Colby, A. (1994). Case studies of exceptional people: What can they teach us? *Journal of Narrative and Life History, 4*(4), 353–365.

Davis, J. M., & Frawley, M. G. (1994). *Treating the adult survivor of childhood sexual abuse: A psychoanalytic perspective.* New York: Basic Books.

Dewey, J. (1938). *Experience and education.* New York: Collier.

Dukes, W. F. (1965). N = 1. *Psychological Bulletin, 64,* 75–79.

English, O. S. (1972). How I found my way to psychiatry. In A. Burton (Ed.), *Twelve therapists: How they live and actualize themselves.* San Francisco: Jossey-Bass.

Erikson, E. H. (1958). *Young man Luther: A study in psychoanalysis and history.* New York: W. W. Norton.

Erikson, E. H. (1969). *Gandhi's truth.* New York: W. W. Norton.

Fenichel, O. (1934). *Outline of clinical psychoanalysis.* New York: W. W. Norton.

Foucault, M. (1961). *Madness and civilization.* New York: Mentor.

Frank, J. D. (1974). Psychotherapy: The restoration of morale. *American Journal of Psychiatry, 131*(3), 271–274.

Frank, J. D. (1979). What is psychotherapy? In S. Bloch (Ed.), *An introduction to the psychotherapies.* Oxford, U.K.: Oxford University Press.

Freeman, M. (1993). *Rewriting the self: History, memory, narrative.* New York: Routledge.

Freud, S. (1950). *Moses and monotheism.* New York: Random House. (Original work published 1939)

Freud, S. (1955). Group psychology and the analysis of the ego. In J. Strachey (Ed. and Trans.), *The standard edition of the complete psychological works of Sigmund Freud* (Vol. 18). London: Hogarth Press. (Original work published 1921).

Freud, S. (1957). Leonardo da Vinci and a memory of his childhood. In J. Strachey (Ed. and Trans.), *The standard edition of the complete psychological works of Sigmund Freud* (Vol. 12, pp. 3–82). London: Hogarth Press. (Original work published 1910)

Freud, S. (1959). Inhibitions, symptoms and anxiety. In J. Strachey (Ed. and Trans.), *The standard edition of the complete psychological works of Sigmund Freud* (Vol. 20, pp. 77–174). London: Hogarth Press. (Original work published 1926)

Freud, S. (1961). Five lectures on psycho-analysis. In J. Strachey (Ed. and Trans.), *The standard edition of the complete psychological works of Sigmund Freud* (Vol. 11, pp. 9–55). London: Hogarth Press. (Original work published 1910)

Freud, S. (1962). The future of an illusion. In J. Strachey (Ed. and Trans.), *The standard edition of the complete psychological works of Sigmund Freud* (Vol. 21). London: Hogarth Press. (Original work published 1927)

Fried, Y. (1978). *Psychopathology: Introductory notes.* Tel Aviv: Ministery of Defence.

Fried, Y. (1984). *Jean Piaget: Psychology and method.* Tel Aviv: Ministery of Defence.

Friedlander, S. (1978). *History and psychoanalysis.* New York: Holmes & Meier.

Fromm, E. (1941). *Escape from freedom.* New York: Farrer & Rinehart.

Fromm, E. (1956). *The art of loving.* New York: Harper & Row.

Fromm, E. (Ed.). (1967). *Socialist humanism—An international symposium.* Garden City, NY: Doubleday.

Gedo, J. (1972). On the methodology of psychoanalytic biography. *Journal of the American Psychoanalytic Association, 20,* 638–649.

Gedo, J. (1983). *Portraits of the artist: Psychoanalysis of creativity and its vicissitudes.* New York: Guilford.

Gergen, K. J. (1988). If persons are texts. In B. S. Messer, L. A. Sass, & R. Woolfolk (Eds.), *Hermeneutics and psychological theory: Interpretive perspectives on personality, psychotherapy, and psychopathology.* New Brunswick, NJ: Rutgers University Press.

Giora, Z. (1988). *The unconscious and the theory of psychoneuroses.* Tel-Aviv: Tel-Aviv University Press.

Giora, Z. (1991). *The unconscious and its narratives.* Budapest: T-Twins Publishing House.

Goldstein, A. P. (1968). An Interview. In A. E. Bergin & H. H. Strupp (Eds.), *Changing frontiers in the science of psychotherapy* (pp. 242–250). Chicago: Aldine Atherton.

Guntrip, H. (1968). *The schizoid phenomena: Object relations and the self.* London: Hogarth Press.

Guntrip, H. (1971). *Psychoanalytic theory, therapy, and the self.* New York: Basic Books.

Habermas, J. (1970). *Toward a rational society.* Boston: Beacon Press.

Hall, C. S., & Nordby, V. J. (1973). *A primer of Jungian psychology.* New York: Mentor Books.

Halleck, S. L. (1971). *The politics of therapy.* New York: Science House.

Heller, D. (1985). *Power in psychotherapeutic practice.* New York: Human Science Press.

Herman, J. L. (1992). *Trauma and recovery.* New York: Basic Books.

Hodder, I. (1994). The interpretation of documents and material culture. In K. D. Norman & Y. S. Lincoln (Eds.). *Handbook of qualitative research* (pp. 393–402). Thousand Oaks, CA: Sage.

Hoffman, L. E. (1982). Psychoanalytic interpretation of Adolf Hitler and Nazism, 1933–1945. A prelude to psychohistory. *Psychohistory Review, 11*(1), 68–87.

Hoffman, L. E. (1984). Psychoanalytic interpretation of political movements, 1900–1950. *Psychohistory Review, 13*(11), 16–29.

Hollis, J. (1993). *The middle passage.* Toronto, Canada: Inner City Books.

Holmes, J., & Lindley, L. (1991). *The values of psychotherapy.* Oxford: Oxford University Press.

Howard, G. S. (1989). *A tale of two stories: Excursions into a narrative approach to psychology.* Notre Dame, IN: Academic.

Howard, G. S. (1991). A narrative approach to thinking, cross cultural psychology, and psychotherapy. *American Psychologist, 46*(3), 187–197.

Jamison, K. R. (1993). *Touched with fire: Manic-depressive illness and the artistic temperament.* New York: Free Press.

Jung, C. G. (1961). *Memories, dreams, reflections.* London: Fontana.

Jung, C. G. (1991). The psychology of the unconscious: A study of the transformation and symbolisms of the libido. In H. Read, M. Fordham, G. Adler, & W. McGuire (Eds.), and R. F. C. Hull (Trans.), *The collected works of C. G. Jung.* Princeton, NJ: Princeton University Press. (Original work published 1912)

Kahn, E. M. (1979, November). The parallel process in social work treatment and supervision. *Social Casework: The Journal of Contemporary Social Work,* 520–528.

Kaplan, H. I., & Sadock, B. J. (Eds.). (1991). *Comprehensive textbook of psychiatry* (Vol. V). Baltimore: Williams & Wilkins.

Kierkegaard, S. (1938). *The journals of Soren Kierkegaard.* New York: Oxford University Press.

Kirschner, S., & Kirschner, D. A. (1993). *Working with adult incest survivors.* New York: Brunner/Mazel.

Kohut, H. (1979). The two analyses of Mr. Z. *International Journal of Psychoanalysis, 60*(3), 3–27.

Kramer, R. (1995). The birth of the client-centered therapy: Carl Rogers, Otto Rank, and "the beyond." *Journal of Humanistic Psychology, 35*(4), 54–110.

Kreisman, J. J., & Straus, H. (1989). *I hate you—don't leave me: Understanding the borderline personality.* New York: Avon Books.

Laing, R. D. (1965). *The divided self.* London: Tavistock.

Laing, R. D. (1967). *The politics of experience.* London: Penguin Books.

Laing, R. D. (1982). *The voice of experience.* New York: Pantheon Books.

Lasch, C. (1979). *The culture of narcissism: American life in an age of diminishing expectations.* New York: Warner Books.

Lifton, R. J. (1973). *Home from the war: Vietnam veterans —neither victims nor executioners.* New York: Simon & Schuster.

Lifton, R. J. (1986). *The Nazi doctors: Medical killing and the psychology of genocide.* New York: Basic Books.

Lifton, R. J., & Stroizer, C. B. (1984). Psychology and history. In M. Borstein (Ed.), *Psychology and its allied disciplines: Vol. 2. The social sciences.* Hillsdale, NJ: Erlbaum.

London, P. (1964). *The modes and morals of psychotherapy.* New York: Holt, Rinehart & Winston.

Mahler, M. S., Pine, F., & Bergman, A. (1975). *The psychological birth of the human infant: Symbiosis and individuation.* New York: Basic Books.

Mair, M. (1988). Psychology as storytelling. *International Journal of Personal Construct Psychology, 1,* 125–138.

Mann, J. (1973). *Time limited psychotherapy*. Cambridge, MA: Harvard University Press.

Marcuse, H. (1964). *One dimensional man*. Boston: Beacon Press.

Marmor, J. (1980). Recent trends in psychotherapy. *American Journal of Psychiatry, 137*(4), 409–416.

Maslow, A. H. (1966). *The psychology of science: A reconnaissance*. New York: Harper & Row.

Masson, J. (1984). *The assault on truth*. New York: Farrar, Straus, & Giroux.

Masson, J. (1988). *Against therapy*. London: Fontana.

McAdams, D. P. (1985). *Power, intimacy, and the life story: Personological inquiries into identity*. Homewood, IL: Dorsey Press.

McAdams, D. P. (1988). Biography, narrative, and lives: An introduction. In D. P. McAdams & L. Ochberg (Eds.), *Psychobiography and life narratives*. Durham, NC: Duke University Press.

McAdams, D. P., & Ochberg, L. (Eds.). (1988). *Psychobiography and life narratives*. Durham, NC: Duke University Press.

McCollum, A. T. (1990). *The trauma of moving*. Newbury Park, CA: Sage.

Menninger, K. (1958). *Theory of psychoanalytic technique*. New York: Harper Torchbooks.

Miller, W. R. (1983). Motivational interviewing with problem drinkers. *Behavioral Psychotherapy, 1,* 147–172.

Miller, W. R., & Rollnick, S. (1991). *Motivational interviewing*. New York: Guilford.

Moraitis, G., & Pollock, G. H. (Eds.). (1987). *Psychoanalytic studies of biography*. New York: International Universities Press.

Murray, H. A., & collaborators. (1938). *Explorations in personality*. New York: Oxford University Press.

Murray, H. A. (1943). *Thematic apperception test*. Cambridge, MA: Harvard University Press.

Murray, H. A. (1981). What should psychologists do about psychoanalysis? In E. D. Shneidman (Ed.), *Endeavors in psychology: Selections from the personology of Henry A. Murray* (pp. 291–311). New York: Harper & Row.

Neumann, E. (1973). *The child: Structure and dynamics of the nascent personality.* London: Maresfield Library.

Noll, R. (1994). *The Jung cult: Origins of a charismatic movement.* Princeton, NJ: Princeton University Press.

Novak, M. (1970). *The experience of nothingness.* New York: Harper Torchbooks.

Patti, R. J., & Resnick, H. (1972). The dynamics of organizational change. *Social Casework, April,* 243–255.

Piaget, J. (1965). *Insights and illusions of philosophy.* London: Routledge & Kegan Paul.

Pinderhughes, E. (1989). *Understanding race, ethnicity, and power: The key to efficacy in clinical practice.* New York: Free Press.

Polanyi, M. (1983). *The tacit dimension.* Gloucester, MA: Peter Smith.

Polkinghorne, D. P. (1988). *Narrative psychology.* Albany, NY: SUNY Press.

Rank, O. (1978). *Will therapy: An analysis of the therapeutic process in terms of relationship.* New York: Norton. (Original work published 1936)

Reich, A. (1951). On counter-transference. *International Journal of Psychoanalysis, 32,* 25–31.

Ricoeur, P. (1970). *Freud and philosophy: An essay on interpretation.* New Haven, CT: Yale University Press.

Ricoeur, P. (1976). *Interpretation theory: Discourse and the surplus of meaning.* Fort Worth, TX: Texas Christian University Press.

Rogers, C. R. (1957). The necessary and sufficient conditions of therapeutic personality change. *Journal of Counseling Psychology, 21*(2), 95–103.

Rogers, C. R. (1961). *On becoming a person.* Boston: Houghton Mifflin.

Rogers, C. R. (1977). *Carl Rogers on personal power.* New York: Delta Books.

Rogers, C. R. (1980). *A way of being.* Boston: Houghton Mifflin.

Rosen, J. N. (Speaker). (1969). *Jim* (Cassette Recording, Tape Library Cat. No. 14). Atlanta, GA: American Academy of Psychotherapists.

Rosenberg, S., & Jones, R. (1972). A method for investigating and presenting a person's implicit theory of personality: Theodore Dreiser's view of people. *Journal of Personality and Social Psychology, 22*(3), 372–386.

Runyan, W. M. (1988). *Psychology and historical interpretation.* New York: Oxford University Press.

Russell, D. (1986). *The secret trauma: Incest in the lives of girls and women.* New York: Basic Books.

Sadock, V. A. (1989). Rape, spouse abuse, and incest. In H. I. Kaplan & B. J. Sadock (Eds.), *Comprehensive textbooks of psychiatry* (Vol. V, pp. 1096–1104). Baltimore: Williams & Wilkins.

Sarason, S. B. (1988). *The making of an American psychologist.* San Francisco: Jossey Bass.

Sarbin, T. R. (Ed.). (1986). *Narrative psychology: The storied nature of human conduct.* New York: Praeger.

Schafer, R. (1981). Narration in the psychoanalytic dialogue. In T. R. Sarbin (Ed.), *Narrative psychology: The storied nature of human conduct* (pp. 129–151). New York: Praeger.

Schafer, R. (1992). *Retelling a life.* New York: Basic Books.

Schofield, W. (1964). *Psychotherapy: The purchase of friendship.* Englewood Cliffs, NJ: Prentice-Hall.

Segal, H. (1964). *Introduction to the work of Melanie Klein.* New York: Basic Books.

Shostrom, E. L. (Producer). (1965). *Three approaches to psychotherapy* [Film]. Orange, CA: Psychological Films.

Siu, R. G. H. (1979). *The craft of power.* New York: John Wiley.

Solomon, M. (1977). *Beethoven.* New York: Schirmer.

Spence, D. P. (1982). *Narrative truth and historical truth.* New York: W. W. Norton.

Sperber, M. (1972). *Alfred Adler oder Das Elend der psychologie.* Tel Aviv: Am Oved. (Original work published 1933)

Stern, D. N. (1985). *The interpersonal world of the infant.* New York: Basic Books.

Stolorow, R. D., & Atwood, G. E. (1979). *Faces in a cloud: Subjectivity in personality theory.* New York: Aronson.

Stroizer, C. B., & Offer, D. (Eds.). (1985). *The leader: Psychohistorical essays.* New York: Plenum Press.

Sullivan, H. S. (1955). *Conceptions of modern psychiatry.* London: Tavistock.

Szasz, T. S. (1968). Interview. In A. E. Bergin & H. H. Strupp (Eds.), *Changing frontiers in the science of psychotherapy* (pp. 241–242). Chicago: Aldine Atherton.

Szasz, T. S. (1978). *The myth of psychotherapy.* Syracuse, NY: Syracuse University Press.

Talley, P. F., Strupp, H. H., & Butler, S. F. (1994). *Psychotherapy research and practice: Bridging the gap.* New York: Basic Books.

Tomkins, S. S. (1979). Script theory: Differential magnification of affects. In H. E. Howe, Jr., & R. A. Dienstbier (Eds.), *Nebraska symposium on motivation: 1978* (Vol. 26, pp. 201–236). Lincoln: University of Nebraska Press.

Tomkins, S. S. (1987). Script theory. In J. Aronoff, A. I. Rabin, & R. A. Zucker (Eds.), *The emergence of personality* (pp. 147–216). New York: Springer.

Toynbee, A. R. (1948). *Civilization on trial.* New York: Oxford University Press.

Wax, J. (1971). Power theory and institutional change. *Social Service Review, 18,* 274–288.

Webb, E. J., Campbell, D. T., Schwartz, R. C., & Sechrest, L. (1966). *Unobtrusive measures: Nonreactive research in the social sciences.* Chicago: University of Chicago Press.

Weinrach, S. G. (1990). Rogers and Gloria: The controversial film and the enduring relationship. *Psychotherapy, 25*(2), 282–290.

White, M., & Epstein, D. (1990). *Narrative means to therapeutic ends.* New York: W. W. Norton.

White, R. W. (1975). *Lives in progress* (3rd. ed.). New York: Holt, Rinehart & Winston.

Whorf, B. L. (1956). *Language, thought and reality: Selected writings of Benjamin Lee Whorf* (John B. Carroll, Ed.). Cambridge, Mass.: MIT Press.

Wolberg, L. R. (1988). *The technique of psychotherapy.* Orlando, FL: Grune & Stratton.

Woolf, V. (1938). *Three guineas.* New York: Harcourt, Brace.

Woolfolk, R. L., Sass, L. A., & Messer, S. B. (1988). Introduction to hermeneutics. In B. S. Messer, L. A. Sass, & R. Woolfolk (Eds.), *Hermeneutics and psychological theory: Interpretive perspectives on personality, psychotherapy, and psychopathology.* New Brunswick, NJ: Rutgers University Press.

Wrong, D. (1980). *Power: Its forms, bases and uses.* New York: Harper & Row.

Name Index

Subject Index